8/6

LETTERS OF GORKY AND ANDREEV

LETTERS OF GORKY AND ANDREEV

1899-1912

EDITED BY PETER YERSHOV

Former Rector
Russian Language and Literature Division
University of Rostov

Routledge and Kegan Paul

LONDON

First Published in 1958
© *by Routledge & Kegan Paul Ltd.*
Broadway House, 68–74 Carter Lane
London, E.C.4
Printed in Great Britain
by T. & A. Constable Ltd.
Hopetoun Street
Edinburgh

ACKNOWLEDGMENTS

WITHOUT the expert guidance of Professor E. J. Simmons and
the efficient help and cooperation of Messrs. Lev F. Magerovsky
and Simeon J. Bolan at the Columbia University Libraries, this
work could never have been completed. The director of the
Research Program on the USSR, Mr. Robert M. Slusser, has
also rendered substantial support. Miss Lydia Weston, who has
translated the Introduction, the Letters, and the Notes, has been
indefatigable as well in checking a number of important
bibliographical items.

PETER YERSHOV

New York
July, 1957

CONTENTS

	PAGE
Introduction	1
The Letters	15
The Notes	147
Bibliography	191
Index	193

ILLUSTRATION

Gorky's handwriting and comic signature   16

INTRODUCTION

INTRODUCTION

A SERIES of letters from Maxim Gorky (Aleksei Maksimovich Peshkov, 1868-1936) to his famous contemporary, Leonid Nikolaevich Andreev (1871-1919), forms the basis of this book. The originals, written in Russian, have been acquired by the Columbia University Libraries as part of their valuable collection of documents and manuscripts in the Archive of Russian and East European History and Culture.

With the exception of a few of the letters previously published in the USSR from copies which Gorky had retained, they have never been printed. Leonid Andreev died in Finland, which after 1918 remained outside the borders of the Soviet Union. Some time after Andreev's death in 1919 the letters were brought by Andreev's heirs to France. They were procured in 1951 by the Columbia University Archive of Russian and East European History and Culture from Mr. Grégoire Alexinsky, in Paris, who apparently acted as agent for the family. For the light they shed on the correspondence, twelve letters from Leonid Andreev to Maxim Gorky which were previously published in Russian in the Soviet Union have also been included in this volume.[1]

Gorky's letters, in many cases, represent much more than a purely personal correspondence: they are often concerned with vital problems of Russian literary and political life from 1899 to 1912. This was an intensely rich period, saturated with historical

[1] Ten of the letters were published in V. A. Desnitskii, ed., *M. Gor'kii: materialy i issledovaniia*, I, 140-78. The two letters written in the spring of 1908 were published in *Literaturnoe nasledstvo*, No. 2 (1932), 105-16. Most of these letters, which were written in 1911 and 1912, are part of the Gorky collection in the Archives of the Institute of Russian Literature of the Academy of Science in Leningrad. Ten letters from Gorky to Andreev, previously unpublished, were published in *Literaturnaia gazeta*, No. 93 (June 18, 1957) Seven are included here.

developments and tragic events. Gorky's letters vividly impart the spirit of that era, the conflict in literary trends which in turn reflected the varied groupings of the divided Russian intelligentsia. The intelligentsia was particularly concerned with reforming or altering the Russian governmental structure and with solving vital social and economic problems relating to the peasantry and the proletariat.

The Russian intelligentsia, including writers and journalists, adhered to widely varying views and political groupings which cannot be crudely divided into a conservative right and a revolutionary left. The political trends of that time were marked by many transitional nuances, reflecting by their instability and mobility the ebb and flow of current events.

After the lull in political and social activity resulting from governmental pressure in the period following the assassination of Emperor Alexander II in 1881, several influential and active political parties arose and grew in strength around the turn of the century. While these parties shared the goal of revolution, they disagreed on methods and programs.[1] There are constant references to this situation in the letters of Gorky, who was a passionate supporter of the "left wing" in the political life of that time.

Gorky began his literary career as a contributor to newspapers. He soon attracted great attention, however, as the first Russian

[1] These parties included: (1) the Socialist Revolutionaries, or SRs, largely successors to the "Land and Freedom" group, later called the "Will of the People," which had been active during the sixties and seventies; (2) the Social Democrats, or SDs, followers of Karl Marx, who in 1903 split into two factions, the Mensheviks and the Bolsheviks. Both the SDs and the SRs sought a revolutionary upheaval in Russia. The SRs especially emphasized the peasant agrarian problem, while the SDs stressed the problem of workers in industry. In addition to these, there existed other parties, among which the Constitutional Democrats, or Cadets, were particularly influential. This party, later known as the "Party of the People's Freedom," was an extensive grouping of liberally inclined intellectuals who wanted to reform the government along parliamentary lines. This group supported revolution only in 1917, when the autocracy was overthrown and a democratic republic was established for a brief interval. The SDs opposed both the SRs and the Cadets.

4

creative writer to depict social outcasts (his enemies called him
the "hobo writer"). The critics were passionate both in attacking
and defending him.

Gorky's excited, bold, sometimes arrogant tone, his penchant
for revolutionary activity, both in literature and in life (participation in underground groups and publishing proclamations
against the government) attracted the sympathies of the student
youth and numerous liberally inclined readers, particularly those
who had not yet espoused a particular party program. His name
had become so popular by 1901 that administrative and police
organs put him under special surveillance and kept systematic
secret records on his conduct. Several times he was subjected to
searches, arrest, imprisonment, or exile to the provinces.

At first Gorky's behavior seemed to be that of a freedom-
loving rebel rather than that of a supporter of any particular
party program. His spirit of revolt attracted great numbers of
readers in the years preceding the first Russian revolution in 1905.
His writings during this period were full of "storm and stress"
but were free of any definite dogma. His undoubted talent,
combined with his persistent and successful efforts at self-educa-
tion, raised him to the first rank of Russian writers. Working
passionately and at the same time restlessly wandering throughout
Russia, he became one of the chief centers of attraction for young
authors.

At the turn of the century Gorky had already begun to influence
the selection of contributions to a number of progressive journals,
particularly the so-called "Legal Marxist" publications *Life* and
God's World. He kept a sharp lookout for talented young writers,
invited their cooperation gladly and without envy, and entered into
a voluminous personal and professional correspondence with them.

In 1898 or 1899 Leonid Andreev, an unknown contributor to
the Moscow newspaper *The Courier*, aroused his interest. Gorky's
artistic sense was not deceived; with his aid Andreev emerged
very quickly as a gifted writer who between 1905 and 1917
attracted a large number of readers in Russia and abroad.

Gorky made the first step toward becoming personally
acquainted with Andreev. He encouraged him, urged him to

intensive, thoughtful creative activity, condemned his hastiness, and frankly criticized his unsuccessful efforts. Nevertheless, Gorky soon came to believe that Andreev's talent was greater than his own.

Andreev's first writings were realistic stories of everyday life, penetrating and precise, exhibiting an original style. His early works seemed to express indirectly a protest against the stagnation of Russian life and petty-bourgeois, conservative self-satisfaction. It was precisely this note of protest which harmonized with Gorky's own beliefs and efforts. In 1901, two years after they became acquainted, Gorky took advantage of his connections with the liberal publishing house of *Znanie* to help speed up the publication of the first volume of Andreev's stories; Andreev dedicated the volume to him. Later stories of Andreev's appeared in the literary volumes published by *Znanie*, which included the works of other young realistic writers, including Bunin, Serafimovich, Teleshov, Kuprin, Chirikov, and Naidenov.

By 1902, however, Andreev had begun to be attracted to themes dealing with psychopathic personalities and "eternal problems," the meaning of life, death, and sexual "mysteries." These themes were an outgrowth, to some extent, of his personal psychopathic condition (chronic alcoholism, which ran in his family), and in Gorky's opinion they turned him away from contemporary problems. Gorky recognized, however, that Andreev's works on such themes were filled with a special charm which had been created by a splendid literary craftsmanship, and, being sensitive at that time to problems of style, language, and composition, he continued to praise his young colleague. He nevertheless kept pointing out to him from time to time the necessity of "coming down to earth" more often, of treating the vital themes of current life, of aiding the revolution by combating the "petty bourgeoisie." Gorky himself considered the terms "petty bourgeois" and "intellectual" to be equally symbols of political inertia and timid liberalism.

Gorky persisted in sharply condemning both the political liberals and the "modernistic" writers who were clustered around the journals *New Path* and *The Scales*. He considered that these writers were contributing to the stagnation of society and were anti-revolutionary; by falling under the influence of Western writers and symbolist poets, he felt, they were distracting Russian readers by obscure and sometimes mystical images and tendencies and were less concerned with content than with the refinements of style.

As the Revolution of 1905 approached, and especially at its height and during his subsequent travels abroad from 1906 to 1913, Gorky became progressively more uncompromising. His materialistic outlook crystallized; he became an atheist (Letter 34). His originally somewhat indefinite "spirit of rebellion" flowed into more disciplined partisan channels. He became a Social Democrat and adopted the revolutionary viewpoint of that party as a guide for the literary activity of himself and his friendly collaborators. He visualized all society as being in the grip of a violent class struggle, in which he supported the proletariat.[1] Andreev, however, becoming increasingly independent and rather intoxicated by the fame which had come to him so soon, grew away from Gorky's influence. This bothered Gorky, who nevertheless continued to regard Andreev as a major artist.

The brief ebb of the tide of revolution in Russia from 1907 to 1912 separated Gorky and Andreev. Gorky lived in Italy, on Capri, where he was a refugee from Russian governmental oppression, having spited the tsarist government by a series of public appearances abroad. Andreev lived in Finland, then a part of Russia, and wrote works which drove Gorky to despair,

---

[1] See Letters 75 and 82, in which Gorky indicates that he had joined the Social Democratic Party. In 1906, Gorky was a delegate to the London Congress of the Party. At Capri he set up something resembling a party school. He developed a close, if not continuous, friendship with Lenin. Gorky's transformation from a rebel into a tendentious revolutionary writer is concretely illustrated in the numerous radical alterations he made in the second edition of his "Song of the Falcon," a nonpartisan hymn to freedom, when it was first published in 1895, but sharply partisan in the 1903 edition (see S. D. Balukhatyi, "Pesnia o sokole," in *M. Gor'kii: materialy i issledovaniia*, III, 161-273). He also made many changes in later editions of his novel *Mother* between 1907 and 1922 in order to intensify its revolutionary ideology (see S. Kastorskii, "Iz istorii sozdaniia povesti *Mat'*," *ibid.*, III, 288-360).

including "Darkness," which in Gorky's opinion slandered the revolutionaries, "My Notes" and *Sashka Zhegulëv*, which, he felt, distorted the facts of the revolutionary movement and the characters of the revolutionaries, and also the plays *The Life of Man*, *Black Maskers*, and *Anathema*, which by their metaphysical themes and symbolic devices identified Andreev with the "modernists," whom Gorky detested.

Their opinions, formerly in agreement, began to diverge sharply; their letters lost their former intimate quality, and the gay jokes and spontaneity disappear. (Some of Andreev's letters to Gorky in the last stage of their correspondence, when both were displaying increasing hostility and misunderstanding, have been published in the USSR; they have been translated and included in this collection.) This divergence was the more tragic as neither could wipe from his memory his sincere affection for the other.

Gorky's former passionateness became intolerance. He lost the breadth of artistic views which he had once had and began to measure the significance of works of art by his own Social Democratic standards. Apparently without noticing it, Gorky became increasingly a revolutionary propagandist and lost some of his power as a creative writer. While abroad after the 1905 Revolution, he wrote works, such as *Mother* and *Life of a Superfluous Man*, which lacked his former freshness and spontaneity; they were the tendentious works of a Social Democrat.

Leonid Andreev, on the other hand, did not surrender his banner as a free artist; he did not submit to any political dogma while analyzing the "cursed" riddles which he sincerely, if unsuccessfully, strove to solve, although he never became a conservative in his view of life.

The conduct of both writers may of course be treated quite primitively, as is done by Soviet scholars: they assert that Leonid Andreev grew frightened, as did other intellectuals, by the revolutionary storm of 1905, while Gorky followed the route of a consistent revolutionary. It appears, however, that the psychological path that each of these writers followed was determined less by revolution than by the dissimilarities of two psychological

8

types. "Les extrêmes se touchent"; two men who were talented, stimulated, impressionable, and sensitive but of sharply divergent temperaments were attracted to each other. Gorky was firmly rooted to the ground and rejected the riddles of existence; he was a utilitarian in art, ready to lend his pen to the service of politics. He surrendered his art completely to politics in the post-revolutionary period and paid heavily for it. Andreev, on the other hand, an alarmed and restless seeker, tried to find out the meaning of life and soared from earth to heaven; he was a metaphysician, indifferent to "ordinary life."[1]

Gorky expressed his annoyance with Andreev in a letter to L'vov-Rogachevskii in 1911 about the latter's article on *Sashka Zhegulëv*:

"What is the basic tendency of all his [*i.e.*, Andreev's] activities? This tendency is the de-socialization of man. Andreev has absolutely no social instinct; he is deeply, zoologically egotistical. . . . [He considers that] life is meaningless and that thus all activity is purposeless. Man is a victim of life, not a constructor of life and not a master."[2]

Gorky expressed the same opinion, although somewhat more mildly, in his reminiscences of Andreev, written after the Revolution.[3] Their divergent political sympathies and principles, their attraction to completely different types of subjects, their

[1] Alexinsky, who knew both writers personally, has expressed a similar opinion (G. Alexinsky, *La vie amère de Maxime Gorki*, pp. 122, 126-27, 131). For an interesting interpretation of Gorky as a disillusioned revolutionist, based on his correspondence with E. D. Kuskova, see her article, "Tragediia Maksima Gor'kogo," *Novyi zhurnal* (New York), XXXVIII, 224-43.

[2] Published in *M. Gor'kii: materialy i issledovaniia*, I, 179-80.

[3] Gorky's article may be found in English in M. Gorky, *Reminiscences of Tolstoy, Chekhov, Andreyev*, pp. 130-88. Lunacharskii, who was very close to Gorky through their Social Democratic activities even before the Revolution, wrote in the preface to two letters from Andreev to Gorky which have been published in the Soviet Union: "Gorky took a lot of trouble over Andreev. He recognized Andreev's great and undoubted talent, but he also felt that this talent was combined with an unusually unstable nature, sick through and through, not only physically but particularly socially" (*Literaturnoe nasledstvo*, No. 2 [1932], 101). For the two published letters, see Letters 81 and 83.

different attitudes toward the technical and aesthetic spects of literary art, and finally their personal misunderstandings were among the reasons for the termination of their friendship. Similar reasons led Gorky to break with others beside Andreev, including Miroliubov and Piatnitskii.

Andreev, for his part, published a denunciation of Gorky's views in 1916.[1] In 1912 their correspondence came to an end. In their creative activity and personal relations, they were irreparably sundered.

The varying course of Gorky's relations with Andreev outlined above is reflected in these letters of Gorky, hitherto unpublished. The letters represent a part of Russian literary history in epistolary form, they record the friendship and misunderstandings of two great Russian writers, and they offer instructive and tragic evidence of how a free artist may be transformed through narrow partisanship into an intolerant propagandist.

The entire collection consists of eighty-four letters and ten telegrams from Gorky to Andreev, one letter from Gorky to a contributor to the Moscow newspaper *The Courier*, asking to make Andreev's acquaintance, and one letter from Gorky's wife, E. P. Peshkova, to Andreev.

Of this collection, eighty-three letters and five telegrams from Gorky to Andreev are published herewith. The collection also includes the first letter in the volume which was written to an acquaintance of Andreev's. One letter from Gorky to Andreev has been omitted because it contains merely a formal greeting. The letter from Gorky's wife to Andreev and a telegram from Gorky to Andreev's wife have also been omitted. Letter 101 from Gorky to Andreev, which was published in the USSR, has been translated and included in this volume for the sake of completeness, although the original is not in the Columbia collection.

Nearly all of the letters were written by hand. Only a few letters, written from 1911 to 1912, are typewritten, with post-

---

[1] Leonid Andreev, "O 'dvukh dushakh' M. Gor'kogo," *Sovremennyi mir*, 1916, No. 1, 108-12.

scripts written in by hand. The reader will find reference to this, as well as explanations of names and events that are mentioned in the letters, in the notes.

Gorky customarily did not date his letters. His handwriting scarcely altered in the interval between 1899 and 1912; it therefore presents no clue for dating. In an effort to reproduce the actual development of the correspondence, these letters have had to be placed in chronological order; this has proved to be a very difficult task, however.

The editor has therefore attempted to establish an assumed or exact date for each letter by the internal evidence of the letters themselves, using as clues references to events, names, journals, newspapers, and so forth. This information, once general knowledge but now requiring painstaking investigation, was compiled; careful study was made of the records of events in the lives of the two writers, including tsarist police records, made when Gorky was being kept under surveillance, published by the Soviet Union. The logical sequence of the correspondence itself was also considered. These furnished the basis for deciding to which period each individual letter belonged. Unless otherwise noted, the dates are Old Style, in accordance with the Julian calendar, which was used in Russia until the Revolution. The old Russian calendar was twelve days behind the Gregorian calendar in the nineteenth century and thirteen days behind in the twentieth.

The following six categories have been established:

1. 1899: two letters and one telegram
2. 1900-1901: 24 letters and one telegram
3. 1902-1903: 22 letters and two telegrams
4. 1904-1906: 26 letters and two telegrams
5. 1907-1909 or 1910: three letters
6. 1911-1912: seven letters

Four telegrams, which have reached us in fragmentary form, and one letter from Ekaterina Peshkova, Gorky's wife, could not be even approximately dated and have not been included in this volume.

These categories demonstrate that the correspondence between the two writers reached its greatest intensity between 1900 and 1906. Particularly strong affection, including the use of the affectionate and familiar term *ty* instead of *vy* for "you," first appears in the correspondence in late 1901 (Letters 26 and 27, see the notes). Several of the letters are interesting as short but illuminating records of Gorky's critical reactions to such important works by Andreev as "Thought" (1902, letter 37), "Red Laugh" (1904, Letter 60), "Lazarus" (1906, Letter 78), *The Life of Man* (1906, Letter 79), "Darkness" (1907, Letter 82), and *Sashka Zhegulëv* (1911, Letter 90). From the text of "Thought," it may be readily seen that Andreev made the changes in language and composition advised by Gorky, although he subsequently paid less attention to his criticisms.

Gorky's two letters from America are of considerable interest (Letters 76 and 77). The first one shows the great impression, favorable in many respects, which American life, and New York in particular, made upon him. The change in his attitude which took place after two or three months may be largely explained by his personal experiences. The hotel where Gorky was staying in New York soon refused him a room because the writer was traveling with a woman to whom he was not legally married. This incident and the subsequent coldness of prominent Americans toward him appear to have affected Gorky's attitude toward America which is reflected in Letter 77. It adds little to his published sketches of the United States, such as "The City of the Yellow Devil."[1]

Because of his partisanship, a number of Gorky's letters produce an unpleasant impression as, for example, his insulting

---

[1] The Soviet Union has given wide circulation to Gorky's hostile reports on the United States during the postwar anti-American campaign; see, for example, *Gorod zheltogo d'iavola* (Moscow: Biblioteka krokodila, 1948), and *V Amerike* (Moscow: Gos. izd-vo Khudozh. lit-ry, 1949). For reports on Gorky's more favourable initial impressions, see Rudolph Zamula, *Maxim Gorky's American Visit and Sketches in Recent Soviet Interpretations* (unpublished Master's essay, Columbia University, June, 1951); for a first-hand account of the visit, see Ernest Poole, "Maxim Gorki in New York," *Slavonic and East European Review*, XXII, No. 58 (May, 1944), 77-83.

references to such highly respected persons as Gol'tsev, Professor Batiushkov, Professor Anichkov, Professor Bezobrazov, and the theatrical director Vladimir Nemirovich-Danchenko.

The places from which the letters were written may only be conjectured in most cases and were even more difficult to discover than the dates. Gorky was an extraordinary traveler and was continuously journeying. While he had a "permanent residence" in Nizhnii Novgorod until 1904 or 1905, he often visited the Crimea, St. Petersburg, and Moscow. The police records for 1902, for example, which were fairly typical for other years in this respect, list no less than fifteen trips. He became more sedentary while an *émigré*, settling down in Capri, where he continued his convalescence from tuberculosis of the lungs which he had contracted in Russia.

Gorky's epistolary style is flexible and varied, ranging in tone from that of polite and refined address, characteristic of his first letters to Andreev,[1] to coarse jokes and scathing attacks. In one case he even wrote a whole letter in blank verse (Letter 57), in which he exhibited considerable facility. The nuances, plays on words, and idiomatic expressions could not always be successfully rendered in the translation; every effort has been made, however, to preserve the meaning of each letter precisely and without distortions. Changes in punctuation have been introduced when they clarify the meaning for the reader.

The letters were written in a precise, round, regular hand, usually on large notepaper, and have been magnificently preserved. A photograph of the opening and conclusion of Letter 57, which was written for the most part in unrhymed trochaic tetrameter, appears on page 16.

[1] See also, for example, Gorky's letters to Professor D. N. Ovsianiko-Kulikovskii, in *M. Gor'kii: materialy i issledovaniia*, III, 135-58.

THE LETTERS

Parts (reduced) of Letter 57, showing Gorky's handwriting and comic signature

I

Nikolai Petrovich![2]

First of all, hello! and secondly, be magnanimous and tell me the address of Leonid Andreev, who has had such wonderful stories published in your paper. Please! It will certainly be very useful to Andreev.

Respectfully,
A. Peshkov

Write immediately to Yalta, Vinogradnaia, Vitmer Villa.

2

(Telegram)

Yalta, April 14, 1899[3]

SEND IMMEDIATELY GOOD STORY YALTA YAKHNENKO HOUSE
TO MIROLIUBOV[4] I WILL BE SATURDAY MOSCOW

GORKY

3

[*Late April (?), 1899*]

It's better to speak without superfluous words. If you, Leonid Nikolaevich, have something ready then please send it to me. I'll try, if it seems possible, to put your things in the *Jour[nal] for All*[5] and in *Life*.[6] I can get them in *God's World*[7] too. I telegraphed you from Yalta to send a story to Miroliubov[8] (that's the editor of *J[ournal]f[or] A[ll]*); have you done it? As for compensation,

I advise you to be modest with this journal; although it only costs a ruble, it has a big income.

You have been writing a year; I, seven. By right of seniority let me give you some advice:

Your stories suffer from lengthiness—you must avoid this. Your language is careless. Pay attention to this. Nowadays the public has become extremely esthetic (this suits it as a rose suits a hog) and very strict. Your best story is "Bargamot and Garaska":[9] long at the beginning, splendid in the middle, but at the end you went off key.

Write, however, as seems best to *you*, as *you* want to write, regardless of praise or censure. Learn compactness and economy of expression from Chekhov, but God prevent you from imitating his language! Chekhov's language is inimitable, and you'll only be spoiled if you court it. It is a beauty who is passionless, and who gives herself to no one. In general, never imitate anyone, but learn only from the great: from Shakespeare to depict sensations, from Turgenev the art of feeling and describing nature, from Chekhov gracefulness in constructing a story.

Please remember this: you yourself must be the sternest and most merciless judge of your works. The writer expresses the spirit of man, the Great Spirit of life, and for him there is no public and there are no idols—nothing except the Spirit. Avoid praise; pay no attention to censure; most of all, fear pleasing yourself. From that day when you feel yourself satisfied, leave off writing, as nothing more that is decent will come out. The self-satisfied man will never create anything necessary for life and for mankind, anything valuable.

Plunge into the business of writing your whole self, your whole personality, and never hesitate to say exactly what you are thinking and feeling, in precisely the words which you find best. Always be sincere.

Forgive the advice. I am young to be teaching. But no one taught me and I have therefore suffered much grief and have made a lot of mistakes. I forced myself and it was so base, so painful. If by my words I have helped you even a little to come out on to the high road, to define yourself, I'd be happy. You have a heart, that's very good; you must suffer a bit and your talent will then become greater than it is. See you soon.

A. Peshkov

Nizhnii. 20 Polevaia Street

4

[Nizhnii Novgorod (?), late 1899-early 1900[10]]

Dear Leonid Nikolaevich!

I am sending your stories. Then you'll return to me "Barga-mot"[11] and "Saburovo,"[12] having given the latter story whatever title you want. I am terribly glad about Posse's[13] proposition and your agreement to work for *Life*. Dear fellow! Treat this seriously, with all the strength and beauty of your soul. How good it would be if you could leave *The Courier* and work freely, whenever you want!

With all my heart I wish you success on your new, fine path. Go forward with all your strength and higher, higher!

Your sincerely affectionate friend,

A. Peshkov

5

[June-July (?), 1900[14]]

I am very much to blame—please forgive me! I liked your "Story about S[ergei] P[etrovich],"[15] although you *can and should* write better, with more form and clarity. I am sure I am not mistaken in thinking you a very talented person.

I have sent the manuscript to the editors of *Life*,[16] and I think it will be published. Although you could still comb it out and smooth it over somewhat. If you want, write the editors of *Life*, at 20 Znamenskaia Street, Evgenii Andreevich Solov'ëv[17] or Vlad[imir] Aleksandr[ovich] Posse[18]—preferably to Posse—and ask them to send you the manuscript or the proofs for corrections. Write where you want me to send your stories. I have lost your address and forgotten your patronymic. Once again I apologize and wish you all the best.

My address: Khoroshki Poltavskoi, Kobeliakskii uezd, Manuil-ovka, to Peshkov.

I am waiting for your answer.

Your A. Peshkov

6

[First half of 1900 *(?)]*

It is one thing to write, but another to be a literary man, Leonid Nikolaevich. I am not yet a literary man, nor are you either, I sense. Therefore, I believe that we shall become closer friends, and I shall take steps toward this.

You wrote a sad letter. All you are going through I also underwent, only I had no one to write to about it. I am offended and hurt that you are sending your story to the *B.V.*[19] competition. Very much hurt. Can't you get along in some way without these thorns? Solov'ëv[20] wrote me of your story[21] that it is written not so much with talent as "neatly and cleverly." Why he's right, that Solov'ëv. Oh, you can write marvellously strongly and vividly! I have read your stories to all types of audiences and have driven them all ecstatic. Look—and by the way we shall speak about it when we meet—"Bargamot and Garaska"[22] must be published in a separate edition. "In Saburovo"[23] also. Let me arrange this, please don't trust it to anyone but me. I'll bring your stories. I shall be in Moscow in a week or something like that. Good-bye, see you soon.

I warmly press your hand.

Your A. Peshkov

7

[Autumn, 1900 *(?)]*

Good Leonid Nikolaevich!

Posse[24] and I must see you. From 4 to 5 today at 84 Bol'shaia Moskovskaia.

A. Peshkov

8

[*September*, 1900 (*?*)]

Good Leonid Nikolae!

Posse[25] and I must see you between 4 and 5 at 84 Bol'shaia Moskovskaia Street today.

A. Peshkov

"The Story about Sergei Petrovich[26] is going in the October *Life*.

9

[*November-December* (*?*), 1900]

Thanks, Leonid Nikolaevich, thanks, my friend! You have written very well of my conflict with the public[27]; you treat it as a *real* writer would. Respect it? Not for anything. Hate it? For everything.

Pek[28] distorted my words. I did not say "You're staring," "Your eyes were wide open," or "Shame!" and—A. P. Chekhov by the way was not there, and I was not drinking tea at the time. But these are details. It will be cleared up. I wish you all the best. I press your hand. Write! Are you working for *Life?*[29]

A. Peshkov

10

[1900 (*?*)]

Leonid Nikolaevich, my good sir!

We have formed a "Society for the Defense of Women"[30] here. We have no funds. We are publishing a volume of stories. Understand?

Write for us, dear fellow, a short story, or write us a big one. You have made a start—splendid! Isn't it about a woman? a prostitute? like "Memorial to Pushkin"?[31] Please, sir, do not refuse—I'll kill you!

No, seriously, when you come here on holiday, bring a little story with you. I'll expect you. I'll expect you even without a story, damn you! Skitalets[32] loves you without having met you and waits, sweetly dreaming of a drinking party together.

Dear fellow, write me a story anyway. And won't you let me know of someone who might be writing an article on prostitution? Isn't Tikhon Polner[33] writing something? If so, send me his address. I will beg from him and pray to him, as I do you. See you very soon!

I warmly press your hand.

A. Peshkov

II

[*Late* 1900 (?)]

Your illness and, particularly, your mood depresses me very much. I don't know you and I don't know why you don't like yourself, why you're so irritated with yourself? I am not a "doctor of souls," but I think lack of self-respect, which I notice in you, results from excessive demands on oneself, and if this is so, then it is good. If only, old man, you would get angry with others instead of with yourself! Then you would have an inexhaustible source of inspiration and you would not treat yourself like an inquisitor. Don't torment yourself; others will torment you. The same Gol'tsev and Co.[34] will give you the devil and will pour all sorts of stupidity and vulgarity on your soul.

It is sad that you are not writing, Lord knows it's sad! I beg you, finish at least one of the four stories you have begun! Dear friend, very few things in this life are as satisfying as work. And I do not understand: why is it shameful to write stories? What is a story? The contents of a soul of a certain man, the views, opinions, joy, grief, love, and hatred of a certain part of the world, since man is a part of the world, and perhaps the whole world. People always need to know what hurts them and what gives them joy, why a certain writer loves them and why he hates their lives. Don't you think I'm lecturing to you, God forbid! I shan't let myself do that. And there is something which I very much like in you—that's why I am getting attached to you.

Oh you rascal! I saw you then, in the theater, with the woman whom you called "your best friend."[35] I looked at you, at her—and envied you. Both were attractive, both were young. I do not know how you feel about her and guessed about nothing. I did not want to, but it was simply pleasant for me to see you with her and her with you. Lovely. Old fellow! Pull yourself together! To hell with your illness, and laziness, and distrust of yourself—these are also sicknesses. And forgive me for this impertinent letter. I am a very clumsy fellow, but a sincere one. I should also add that in my sincerity I sometimes act like the butt end of an ax. Now I don't think I've made any such blunder?

I press your hand warmly and wish you boldness of spirit.

And if you leave *The Courier*,[36] it will lose a great deal, but you won't.

Good-bye, I shall be waiting for you impatiently until Christmas. I shall send you a bridegroom's wedding mask.

A. Pesh

12

[Late 1900–early 1901 (?)]

My dear Leonida!

Thanks, but—I'm sorry.

I'm sorry that a "writer" was distributed in this publication,[37] when there is another, cleaner one.

The remark about the point of departure is correct, I know that myself. Don't connect this incident with the theater.[38]

Skitalets[39] sings, "I shall le-e-e-ead the bride!" She has been at our house once, but not twice.

I hug your belly—

A. Pesh

13

[Nizhnii Novgorod, late 1900–early 1901 (?)]

My very good, wayward fellow!

Thanks for your promise to write a story for our volume![40] Does that mean that the matter is settled? Well, fine.

Drag, beg, urge Kaufman[41] and Alekseevskii.[42] We'll put together such a book that it will knock them flat and that's all there'll be to it![43]

Chirikov[44] will give us a splendid story. In general, it is a matter either of "bust our prick or split a cunt." We shall put this wise saying in the volume as an epigraph.

I am waiting for you with all my might. Come to see me although in my house it is as cold as Spitzbergen (where I have never been, by the way). Skitalets[45] thirsts for you and has even stopped drinking vodka in anticipation. I also am not drinking. I am waiting.

Old man, I'll show you my Christmas tree for a thousand children.[46] It will be a good Christmas tree, may the devil eat you!

Come soon. Bring your best friend too. We shall go to parties, we shall talk, in general, "we'll drink, love the lassies, and then go begging! Ah, take a thread from all the world, and there'll be a noose for the poor man. And if you escape the noose, your own guts will choke you."[47]

I press your hand.

A. Peshkov

14

[*Probably Nizhnii Novgorod, mid-February-April (?), 1901*]
My dear Leonidushka!

I am enclosing a little anecdote not approved by the censor here. If Fagin[48] wants, he can publish it in *The Courier,* and it would be good on St. Thomas's Sunday.[49] Hm, yes.

And "Once upon a Time"[50] is splendid! You, my little fellow, are an extremely good boy. Your spirits are rising. I don't want you to marry anyone.

Your friend and well-wisher,

A. Peshkov

15

[*Nizhnii Novgorod (?), late* 1900-*early* 1901 (?)]

Well, you are a good boy.

Tell me where to send you money and such things.[51] Why loll about for nothing? Write a good story for *Life*[52] and take a rest from *The Courier*.[53]

Don't you know N. I. Timkovskii's[54] address? I want to get a story from him for the volume. Bye—see you soon!

Will you be lying around long? When will I get stories? As for this last matter, tell me your wishes in detail. Addio!

A. Peshkov

16

[*Nizhnii Novgorod (?), late* 1900-*early* 1901 (?)]

Don't grieve, old fellow, all Russians have rotten hearts. You'd do better to tell me whether you got the 500 rubles?[55] It was time. Get well soon. That's all.

Your A. Peshkov

I'll get the stories from your house when I come, understand?

17

[*St. Petersburg (?),*[56] *late February-early March,* 1901[57]]

I am well, and in my heart the spring's sunbeams are shining, and I breathe with my whole chest. I might even fall in love, but there's no object for this, but if there were an object—ah, how I would fall in love! right down to ashes! neither she nor I would be left, only a few bones, a tiny bit of skin, and—two piles of ashes. And all the rest, soul, mind, strength, would be consumed by love.

To hell with Filipov![58] I wrote something a little while ago about a stormy petrel,[59] and I wrote it, and I'm publishing it, and then all the Gol'tsevs[60] will say that I am imitating Filipov.

Now you come here! On the 8th we'll have a demonstration[61] here, by God!

On the second or third day of Easter week I'll be in Moscow, perhaps at your house. Although I am actually going to see Tolstoy. Did they write you something from *Znanie*[62] about the book? No? Then you ask me about it—I also know nothing about it. But I shall know, damn you! Write, dear fellow, something in the spirit of "In the Dark Distance."[63] I ask it in Christ's name! Write, as such stories *now* are needed as much as bread, as air, as wine and woman.

I embrace you. I might embrace the sun if necessary.

Ever yours,
A. Peshkov

It is good to live on earth!

Truly on earth it is good to live, my dear comrade. Look, I want to give you some sort of present but I haven't a cent. So buy yourself Lichtenberger's book *The Philosophy of Nietzsche*[64] in Popova's[65] edition and imagine I gave it to you. And I'll give you something later. All right?

18

(Telegram)

March 1, 1901

SEND ANY STORIES READY

DEACON PESHKOV[66]

19

[Nizhnii Novgorod, 1901 (?)]

Come here, old man—it's inconvenient and extravagant to write letters, an awful lot of dough goes for stamps. Come by railway, and bring your new story.

We'll talk, and we'll see. And the "desperately enterprising man"[67] can't come? He might.

Well, what of the play? We need the play. I'll soon begin a

26

second,[68] since it is fully obvious to me that the first is not fit for anything.

I am so stirred up in general about drama that now—Take care, William Shakespeare! Tremble, Nestor Kukol'nik![69] Nothing will stop me now!

You may print in *The Courier*[70] that Gorky has devised a new drama from the era when the Jews crossed the Red Sea. The basic idea is that for a drunk man the sea is actually up to his knees, and not more, as sensible people assert.

Well, both the sea and the Jews are trifles in comparison with one idea. And this is what it is: you are a belletrist. I'm the *Nizhnii Novgorod News.*[71] I want some good creative writing. But with my means I can't pay more than three kopecks for it. Well?

I say to my neighbor the *Northern Land*[72] and to my neighbor the *Volga Herald*[73] and to my neighbor the *Samara Gazette*[74] and to another Saratovite: "Brothers! Shall we publish good writing at three kopecks a line?" They ask, "But how?"

And this is how: *we all will publish on* one *and the same day* a story by L. Andreev or M. Gorky and will all give them, the rascals, three kopecks each. Then we'll have Andreev for three kopecks apiece, and he'll get from us fifteen kopecks a line! Simple, clear, and not bad. The five papers have 20,000 subscribers, at least. It would be worth something to appear before such an audience. But my dear friend! silence! If someone sneaks this idea, I'll sue you for a loss of 2,397,862,356 rubles. A fact!

Good-bye!

I'm expecting you with all your retinue.

A. Peshkov

20

[*Nizhnii Novgorod, May–September*, 1901 (?)[75]]
Your letter reached me and brought me much satisfaction. Might I read your bit of a story?[76] And publish it—either right away in *Russian Riches*,[77] or if you'd like to borrow two hundred rubles from me on this story, then we'd hide it for a while, for

a time. We'd either publish it in a volume or in our journal,[78] which should be . . .

Dear friend, find out two things for me in Moscow: first, when and why is the journal *Truth*[79] to be published and who is publishing it? . . . and secondly, who is Vladimir Sablin[80] and why is he thinking of publishing a "journal of creative literature and the theater"?

Mother in heaven! Soon there'll be two publishers for every writer!

I am living in my old apartment. Write my wife. I'm expecting *Stories* any day. No time to write. I liked Shaliapin[81]—beyond all bounds.

Your A. Peshkov

My wife says: "that he won't send me his picture, I'd like to look at it. Write him." I wrote him.

And I signed: A. Peshkov.

21

[Nizhnii Novgorod, late September-early October 1901]
The book[82] is delectable. It is real literature.

You're a fine fellow. I read the whole book and drank a bottle of wine worth three silver rubles to your health. Then friends came in, they read and drank some more to Russian literature.

Ah Leonidushka! My friend! This is a good job, to be a writer, especially good to be a writer in Russia, and therefore, brother, it's good that it is very vile. And in general it's a great pleasure to live on earth and I can't imagine a more splendid occupation.

A play? splendid! Amazingly good, and precisely on that theme! You must write! You must want to write and you'll write. You're a talented animal, you'll write! I feel this. But beware of being clever. It is enough to be talented, to write well, and you must know the smell of human blood, tears, and sweat. You must hate unhappiness, not overindulge the unhappy. You understand all this. "The Story about S[ergei] P[etrovich]"[83] is a good, clever, fine piece. Imagine! I didn't like it before, and now I just read it again and said "aha!" And "On the River." "On the River" is very good. Yes, sir! I am terribly pleased and gay, for you are a glorious person! You'll write a play and many more significant, worth-while works. This is a fact. You love the sun. This is splendid, this love is the source of true art, of real poetry, of that poetry which makes life live. And as for me, I've become cleverer, and since then my talent has been getting dull. But that's nothing. You've had a wonderful idea—get on with your play.

Sablin[84] came. He's a clumsy lout. But we'll try and see what he'll do. I told him that you had a story and that you need money. He seemed to understand. Well, I wrote a play.[85] It's bad. It is shrill, vain, and empty. Never mind! I'll write another.

I want very much to see you.

Bezobrazov[86] came. He invited me. I refused. I have rarely met such a stupid person as he, and never did I see a more boorish professor. The journal he started will be his grave, a disgrace. Well, the Lord be with him! I love to see a man doing something silly, seriously, and with love.

I warmly press your hand,

A. Peshkov

I told the government that I can go to Arzamas[87] only by stages, and I won't go on order. If they are embarrassed at sending me with a guard, I'll win. If they aren't, I'll also win. So that's the way it is!

22

[Nizhnii Novgorod, October, 1901[88]]

Dear Leonidushka!

Don't talk nonsense.

Congratulations on the publication of your book. You could send the story both to Brusianin,[89] after asking an advance from him, and to the R[ussian] R[iches],[90] saying that I advised it, that is, that I advised you to send it. *RR* (*RR* [RB] does not by any means stand for "fish" [*ryba*] but for *Russian Riches*) doesn't give advances. I also won't send you money because I don't have any money! That's strange, but it's a fact. A laughable, tangible, tragic fact. By the way, how can nonexistence be a tangible fact?

You, sir, will get 1200 rubles as income from your book, but whether this includes the 500 ruble advance or not I don't know. Brusianin is a fine lad. I'm not dragging you into anything. The proof is the enclosed letter. Out of friendship for me, couldn't you break one or two ribs for that kind gentleman who wrote in *The Courier* that my health leaves nothing to be desired? One is exiled to Arzamas,[91] one sends a request to the Minister, stating that my illness requires me to go not to Arzamas but to Yalta, and—all of a sudden! Why always be telling the truth? It's dull, it's dangerous, and in general, I don't like it.

You fellows on *The Courier* have done me a bad turn! If you'd like to come and see me it would be a very good deed on your part.

May the W.B.* protect you and have mercy upon you.

A. Peshkov

* W.B. in Russian is the Wild Boar. Full title of the W.B.: His Supreme Excellency, the Director of the Secret Society, with the trade name of the Ministry of Internal Affairs.

23

[*Nizhnii Novgorod, October 25, 1901*]

Received permission to go to Yalta; going around November 10th. I'll plead for a chance to stay several days in Moscow, but don't let this reach the newspapers.

Today, in the *Nizhnii Novgorod News*[92] of the 25th, there is an article by Iarovitskii-Kornev[93] "On the Stories of L. Andreev." Not bad. Kornev is the author of the story "Husband of Duty."

A. Peshkov

24

[Nizhnii Novgorod, before November 8, 1901]

Lenichka!

News! Vl[adimir] Iv[anovich] Nemirovich-Danchenko,[94] who is staying with me, told me that on the road from Moscow to Nizhnii he had discovered a new and very talented creative writer, a certain L. Andreev. Thereupon I told him that this Leonid is really someone! And that he, Leonid, wants to write plays. Of course, both of us became exultant.

Now I must introduce you, my sweet, to this same Vladimir Ivanovich. I must, I know this, and he knows it too. He is an intelligent man, sincere, with taste, and knows theatrical work as I know baker's work. No, better than I know baker's work. You'll get acquainted. You must. Nemirovich-Danchenko may be very useful.

Sabler[95] told me about "The Wall,"[96] not very clearly. And I haven't seen it, haven't received it, and haven't read it. I'm waiting.

I have taken the preliminary test for the rank of dramatist.[97] What will the state examination say?

A. Peshkov

Am I signing my last name well?

25

[Nizhnii Novgorod, early November, 1901]

Dear Leonid Nikolaevich!

Tell Iakov Abramovich (?) Fagin[98] the following: shortly Stanislav Ivanovich Grinevitskii, the editor of the *Nizhnii Novgorod News*,[99] will send him the manuscript of my story. It will be material for two or three *feuilletons*. My one condition is: that the story should be begun in *The Courier* on the very same day as in the *News*, not before. Only on this condition, strictly observed, will I publish in *The Courier*. The fact that the same story will be published simultaneously in two publications will of course lower the fee for it and therefore let *The Courier* pay me at the five-kopeck rate or—how much does it usually pay for original creative writing to writers who are not original?

Here it is. Grinevitskii will set the day and the stories will come from him. About the play,[1] the anthology, and other wounds of the heart I won't speak now. Sablin[2] was here. I promised him a play. Then, there was still another lover of drama. I almost promised him one too. I also promised you. That I remember. I shall clarify this: one shouldn't promise people plays, for once they want to have one the author is placed in the dramatic position of either giving them all one act each or shooting them all and strangling himself. I am beginning to think that I can avoid offending every one only by giving nothing to any one.

I, my dear friend, am tired, half-sick, and as upset as a nervous old woman. My head aches, and at night my heart is acting up. At first it beats very rapidly, and then it gets tired, and then it seems not to be working at all. And at such moments I think: and what if I pop off, I, Peshkov? That's nonsense, of course, I know, I won't pop off for a long time, but you know what these irregularities are like and how they affect the imagination.

And by the way—good-bye!

I am leaving for Yalta on the 7th.[3]

A. Peshkov, who won't pop off yet!

26

[*Koreiz, Crimea, November–December,* 1901]

Friend Leonid!

Please send me *The Courier* to the address
Koreiz, Tauris Province,
Oleiz, c/o Tokmakov
A. M. Pesh

Here the sea is damp, the sky is damp, the land is damp. I drink a lot of wine. Come, although it's dull. My place is big; there's space to live. What happened to that Tolstoy which they wanted to present to me? They say it was taken away and that students have been beaten; is it true?[4] If it's true, it's offensive.

Well, friend, good-bye!

It would be very human if various people would from time to time communicate to me what is happening in Russia.

A. Pesh

27

[*Crimea* (?), 1901 (?)]

How many beggars there are in Russia, Leonid! When I read the papers I hear their mournful, servile howl:

"Your Supreme Excellency! Sacrifice to the much-suffering Russian press at least a little bit of freedom of speech and it will preserve your double name in the memories of succeeding generations from age to age!"

Good-bye, friend! It is very good that you[5] and I are friends, isn't it?

A.

28

[*Crimea* (?), *late* 1901–*early* 1902 (?)]

Dear old Leonid!

You try, together with Gavrilych,[6] or collectively, to write Fëdor[7] a formal congratulatory letter. Please! The fact is that I don't have time to wipe my nose.

Tomorrow, probably, K.P.[8] will send off your payment.[9] You may have 400 rubles net, and more, a month for ten months and even for a year. Is it enough? K.P. will explain this book-keeping in detail.

Aleksei

29

[*Moscow* (?), 1902 (?)]

Kon[stantin] Petr[ovich][10] arrived. He wanted to drop in on you but couldn't, as Bunin[11] was to come to see him and Serafim[ovich][12] to see me. Won't you show up here? Appear, you son of a bitch! And bring what you have written about Fëdor.[13]

A.

30

[*Crimea, early* 1902][14]

I got a letter from Piatnitskii.[15] You sent him "Alarm,"[16] "Laughter,"[17] "In the Basement."[18] They make 1½ signatures. He needs five signatures to put a price of one ruble on the volume.[19] I also sent him "The Abyss,"[20] which I read aloud yesterday with pleasure to guests. It will make a tremendous impression. You're a fine fellow.

Send Piatnitskii "Petka"[21] too. And "The Student"[22]—is it ready? And "Thought"?[23] And "Mutiny on Shipboard"?[24] Friend, we must get together three more signatures. Otherwise the public will curse us. For it, literature is worth less than twenty cents, remember this.

Your A. Peshkov

Hurry, the book is being published.

Come soon! I'll put you and your wife up beautifully. We have champagne, priests too.

You're ill? Then come here, you odd fellow! Here there is the sun, the sea, and the almond trees are in bloom. Isn't it all the same where you marry?[25] What is important is how?

31

[*Koreiz, Crimea, early* 1902]

Dear friend!

I beg you, read the enclosed piece and tell me how you like it? Its author, a good young man, sent you three of his things and now is asking me about their fate. Write him or me. His name is Aleksei Vasil'ev Iarovitskii,[26] his address *Nizhnii Novgorod News*. I think he's very talented; he has written some really wonderful things. I got your volume; it was ridiculous for the bookbinder to stick such big words on the back. For the inscription,[27] I thank you and—I reject it. You know, Schopenhauer has a

34

wonderful aphorism: "Modesty is a value only to the man who has no other values." Value yourself more highly: you won't be prevented from growing and broadening, and it will give your companions a fortunate opportunity and great pleasure to give you hell for it.

And forgive me! the devil knows why, but I keep wanting to give you advice! I must be getting old.

Don't write so hastily as you wrote "In the Basement."[28] In counting over stories for the second edition[29] I forgot two wonderful ones, "Kusaka"[30] and "The Event"[31]

Read Ganeizer's[32] sketch, "The Bewitched Streetlamp," in *The Petersburg Herald*, and if you understand what is going on here and why it was written, tell me. Ganeizer's familiarity struck me very unpleasantly; why am I "Aleksei Maksimovich" to him? I know him, or rather I have seen him, but I can say of him only one thing: that he is the husband of Julia Bezrodnaia,[33] the writer. What will happen to Russian literature if the writers start beginning stories like this: "Having killed his wife, the craftsman Peshkov, well known in literature as Maxim Gorky, wearily lowered himself into a chair and said, sighing with relief: 'How I sweated! But—never mind! The Lord loves labor.'" Or "'James Lynch,'[34] the same as Leonid Andreev, walked drunk into the editorial offices of *The Courier*, and, belching, cried to the whole street: Hey, you Ganeizers! All come out at once!"

Piquant. But hell! Something's wrong here, but I can't quite pin it down!

Well, good-bye for the present! I'm eagerly waiting for you.

Your A. Pesh

If you told Fagin[35] to invite Kornev[36] to participate in *The Courier*, it wouldn't be a bad idea. Kornev must be brought into "society"; help me do this. I'm sure that he'll write well.

Tell Fagin, by the way, to send me money and that I'll send him some allegory immediately.

Koreiz, Tavr. guberniia
Oleiz, etc.

32

[*Moscow (?),*] *April* 14, [1902][37]

Alekseiushko dear—when you've read "Thought,"[38] send it right back to me. This is the reason: Miroliubov[39] was here and said that *Russian Riches* needs creative writing very much, and Mikhailovskii[40] is strongly urging me to contribute something. Then Miroliubov gave me his opinion on the relative advantages of *God's World*[41] and *Russian Riches*, mentioned how proper Korolenko[42] is (did you know he left the academy?) and came to the sound conclusion that I should send "Thought" to *Russian Riches*, not to *God's World*. And I agree with him completely, but:

(1) We don't know whether Mikhailovskii will like the basic idea of the story.

(2) I've gotten an advance from *God's World;* 200 rubles.

(3) Bogdanovich[43] has repeatedly asked me for the story and I promised it to him and mentioned that it would be called "Thought."

(4) At the end of April, I want to give *Russian Riches* a story about a priest ("Arise and Walk").[44]

Therefore in about four days I'm going to St. Petersburg, I'll read "Thought" to Mikhailovskii, and if he likes it very much I'll offer it to him and I'll give Bogdanovich the priest. I'll lie my way out of this somehow.

Now tell me, do you approve all this or not? I think you're on the side of *Russian Riches*, and that's why I'm planning to act so decisively.

Send the story to me at the following address: Moscow, B. Gruzinskaia, c/o Perelman. Write.

I warmly press your hand.

Your Leonid Andreev

33

[*Crimea, early* 1902][45]

My fine friend!

If there is talk of "sham renown," it must mean they are beginning to get envious; *ergo* (as the Latins used to say) soon

they will begin to hate you. And hatred for the good writer is
pepper, mustard, and other essential seasoning for cooking up the
impressions of life. I would very much like them to hate you,
even a lot, because, you see, each time the nose of my soul smells
the smell of hatred it makes me cleverer and more talented, and
you need this smell too. And you need it even more than I
do. Because I have had a whiff of glory (glory smells bitter in
Russia!) and you have not yet. Fear praise especially, oh Leonid!
Each time I hear praise it seems to me that it comes from the
lips of a son of a bitch, and that he praises me because he is
afraid, the poor creature, that I might have told the truth about
him. The praise of the Russian man on the street, who is
accustomed to bribing everyone, from the patrolman to God, is
suspicious.

Don't let this advice offend you, friend and comrade. I say
again: youth loves you for the present on credit, since you, sir,
have not given it anything yet except for "Dark Distance."[46]
These days youth is demanding joyous, heroic, and romantic
stuff (in moderation). And (I'm serious) you must write something in this vein. Anyway Russia is going through a revolution,
not the kind where there is fighting in the streets and kings'
heads are cut off, but another more serious kind. The philosophical and ethical basis on which the welfare of the petty
bourgeois depends is in decay. The enemies now are not only the
Gringmuts,[47] Meshcherskiis,[48] and Co., so much as the plaster
which cements the cracks in the old shed of our life, i.e., Messrs.
Men'shikov,[49] Rozanov,[50] Merezhkovskii,[51] Russians from
Russian Word, and others of this honorable spirit, who could
be called the "riffraff of Christ." Not of the real Christ, but of
that church-policeman who recommended dedication to God
and the tsar, equally. Although I would approve the real Christ
if He would hurry to appear. His time will be in about a thousand
years from now, not until after we plot with each other, fight,
and get tired. And when we do get tired, then we will begin to
make love to one another because you know it is most convenient
to do *this* lying down. That means, beat the preacher of love
Men'shikov, for the very reason that he preaches love, the

scoundrel, so that his life might not be disturbed by the tragedy of his contradictions. Beat the petty bourgeois! since he likes to put up fences everywhere. But I am probably boring you.

I wrote Teleshov.[52] The thing is wonderful. Send your book to Evgenii N. Chirikov,[53] Iaroslavl', that's all. If you need money, ask Piatnitskii[54] whether he has any of yours, and if not ask him for some of mine. Write him: "I'm getting married!" and he'll give you some. When you're married, come. I'll lock you up here in a comfortable place and you'll write, and your wife will go walking. I don't know her, but her face and eyes are lovely. I hope she has character and will take you in hand.

"Alarm"[55] is splendid! Very splendid. But if Benvenuto Cellini had begun to make only brooches for ladies and tie pins for cavaliers, I would have had to hit Benvenuto with a stick on the head. Forgive me, brother! You must spread out further, jump higher. "Alarm," I say, is amazing! But "Wall"[56] with all its gloom promised something more. Send "Thought"[57] to *Russian Riches*, by God! It is said that N. K. Mikhailovskii[58] *himself* has written about you. This, friend, doesn't happen to every one, and although it happened with me it was not particularly pleasant for me. Mikhailovskii's voice, although it is not ridiculous and not inept, is unnatural and little heard now, but he himself is a deserving man, etc. Send it to him. There's good company for Murav'ëv:[59] Andreev, Chirikov,[60] Shestov,[61] the author of the book *Good in the Teachings of Tolstoy and Nietzsche,* Nevedomskii,[62] the author of the preface to Lichtenberger's book[63] and of articles in *Nachalo*, Vasilii Iakovlevich Bogucharskii,[64] the writer Serafimovich,[65] of course Posse,[66] and who else? I don't remember now. Posse, for your information, is a wonderful lad. He is intelligent, an organizer, a warm heart, capable of attracting any man. I am very sure that if you meet him you will love each other sincerely and strongly.

Well, now do this, my friend. Get money from Fagin[67] and buy me *Notes of Volkonskii*, the Decembrist, and when you have bought it send it to me. Quickly, please. Get more money and have your book bound and send it to me too. I need this. You lash up this book for me and I'll lash into you later. . . . Greetings

38

to the bride. Bride or Bridde, how do you spell it? Don't remember.

So you'll come? I'm waiting for you.

A. Peshkov

Boom! A telegram from Kiev: an old friend of mine, Nikolai Vasil'ev,[68] an old laboratory worker at the Polytechnic Institute, got poisoned and died. My wife is going to Kiev. This is a terrible blow for me. A rare man has died, a rare man.

34

[Crimea, early 1902]

Don't give up! I promised at random.

One question that you're thinking about—to write or not to write?—is clearly answered: to write for *this* journal[69] is not worth while for you, and you won't write well for it.

And for such publications it is essential (contrary to generally accepted custom) to write as well as possible. I advise you: in this matter wait until you yourself want to write, until your soul is not torn.

You wrote well about "The Three,"[70] although you are not a critic. But you didn't understand Il'ia as I understand him. Il'ia does not repent before the people, but speaks to them in scorn. As a judge over himself he cannot accept either the people, whom he himself condemned, nor God, whom he has lost.

There is no God, Leonidushka. There is a dream about Him, there is an eternal, dissatisfied yearning in one way or another to explain to oneself oneself and life. God is a convenient explanation of all that is taking place around us, and that's all. Tolstoy, who appears to believe in God, really is preaching the necessity for some sort of pantheistic hypothesis. For the present God is not required, since if we grant Him the shopkeepers will immediately hide behind Him from life. Now, God is slipping away from the shopkeepers, and the sons of bitches are left without a shelter. That's how it must be! Let them jump about in life naked with their empty little souls and moan like cracked bells. And when they die from cold and spiritual starvation we'll create a God for ourselves who will be great, splendid, joyous, the protector of life who loves everyone and everything. So be it!

And we wouldn't give God to the shopkeepers, even if He existed.

Get married[71] fast and come. Don't sulk, but work. If you're bored, don't go to see people, they won't entertain you, but sit down and write, write, write—it doesn't matter what, so long as it's done sincerely. By God!

Very anxious to see you.

Get money from Fagin[72] and buy with it the book of *Miroliubov*,[73] *on Sakhalin*, and send it to me immediately. I need it very much. And don't go to Vik[tor] Miroliub[ov][74] at the *Journal*. Don't go—I speak sincerely! To write you must write and not go out.

See you soon.

Al. Pe

35

[Crimea (?), first half of 1902 *(?)]*

I am definitely in favor of setting the price of one ruble on the booklet after supplementing it.[75] This is an advantage for you, believe me. "Alarm," "The Abyss," "Laughter," "The Wall," "Petka," "Kusaka"—that, perhaps, is enough for a ruble. And as for the buyer, let him buy twice! To hell with him anyway. Ask Piatn[itskii][76] immediately: are six stories enough? I forgot "In the Basement." It will be enough!

Are you "an organic pessimist"? An interesting discovery. I am very much obliged to Mr. Shkliar'![77]

Your story about the ikon[78] is splendidly conceived, amazingly truthful in its plot, heavy at the end (as it is in reality), and—uncensorable. Don't be upset by this, though, but go on at full speed! Write it and—hide it. When you and I abolish the censor we'll publish it.

It appears that there are seven stories! Well, I think that's enough. Act quickly, don't delay!

Don't look for any Miroliubov,[79] you needn't; Miroliubov isn't a store but the author of a book, *Sakhalin*, and I have already read it, a fate which I won't wish on you.

A. Pe

36

[*Crimea, early* 1902]

Friend!

I got your three letters. Are you married yet or not?[80] I'll congratulate you when you come here, but now I keep thinking: how well some time you'll write your memoirs: "How I got married." How did it happen that you had to give a signed promise not to leave? What for?

And that's good, my friend, for a Russian writer should never live in friendship with the Russian government. It doesn't matter what kind it might be: autocratic, constitutional, or—even!—republican. . . . As in all three forms, ours will be—by its very essence—equally trashy. Therefore, government by Philistines.

Well, fine, we won't talk of politics, since if we do it may become viler than it is. Here's the story: on the 23rd to the 24th, *i.e.*, on the same day as you, Doctor Alexander Aleksin,[81] my friend, is coming to Yalta from "Florence" on Tverskaia. Join up with him! He's an interesting beast.

Addio!

A. Pesh

37

[1902]

The story[82] is good. Leonid Andreev is his own master in the regions of the unknown, and the gulfs of black mysteries are visited by him as easily and freely as the bars of the common people are visited by Skitalets.[83] Nothing! "And in iron hearts: beat! that is the meaning of all philosophy!" Let it be horrible for the petty bourgeois to live, fetter his filthy wantonness with iron links of despair, pour horror into his empty heart! If he can bear all this, he'll get well, and if he can't he'll die, and disappear—hurrah!

But of all this later. The story has been sent, you'll get the proofs. Look carefully at the fourth page to see if you don't find something superfluous there. It's somewhat long; it seems there are repetitions. Then: my friend! you must cut or rework the end. You must. Let the ending be several lines long, with the terrible word "NOTHING" in the chief place. "When, in court, the judge turned to the accused, etc., Dr. Kerzhentsev looked at him, at the public, at everything with apparently blind, cold eyes and calmly —calmly!—said—'NOTHING!'"

Believe me, friend, that word should be the last word of the story, precisely that word! The jurors, the court audience, the questions—all is superfluous! They are all trifles. Think about it!

I cannot write more convincingly, and I won't write any more. I warmly press your hand, very warmly. Greetings to your wife.

A. Peshkov

Yes, I forgot! The third edition[84] is being printed, the second was sold out. The third will be 10,000 copies. Come into *Znanie* as a shareholder, you really should! The money will be more intact and you will have a voice in the business of furnishing the market with books.

38

[*Arzamas, May–August*, 1902]
Office and File Room of the Publishing Company
Znanie
St. Petersburg, 92 Nevskii Prospect
. . . . . 1901[85]

Write me a letter to Arzamas, and I'll answer you. You rascal, you were to send me your book in a good binding, and you didn't send it! Shame on you!

For that I am bestowing on you Cheops' pyramid; wear it instead of a hat. Don't thank me, it's not worth it! Are you writing? Write! I'm writing. Although the inks are bad, write! It's pleasant here, friend.

A. Peshkov

39

[Nizhnii Novgorod (?), mid-1902 (?)]

I sent you K.P.'s[86] letter, in which he proposes to issue "Thought"[87] in a separate edition. To this I added my advice: not to listen to Piatnitskii, and not to publish "Thought" separately. Where are you hurrying to? And why give the rogues an opportunity to be malicious?

Why don't you send me books, you rascal! It's bad! Hurry, please! Greetings to your wife. Work!

Good-bye!

Skitalets[88] is coming here.

A. Peshkov

40

[Moscow, September, 1902]

Leonidushka!

Now we are going to Eliseev's house for a discussion and don't know how long it will last. We stayed at 24 Moskovskaia Street. Tomorrow at 12 o'clock we'll be at Skirmunt's.[89] If you can't pay a visit today because of your head, then—please!— come tomorrow toward 12 to Granatnyi Lane. K.P.[90] will be there too. I'm expecting you today too.

Aleksei

41

(Telegram)

[Crimea, November 17, 1902 (?)][91]

READ IT[92] OUR CONGRATULATIONS GOOD

SKITALETS   PESHKOV

42

[1902 (?)]

My dear Leonid!

I too have long been sick of this heavy and sad business,[93] and if you hadn't written me I would have written you soon anyway.

Don't think that you have made any "first step." I warn you, because I know the strength of that furtive sensitivity which is called human pride.

First of all, tell your wife that I have felt guilty about her all this time, and I do now. She will understand why. I remember very well her glance at my mug when we (you, she, and I) met on the shore at Yalta. In general, the worst thing about this business was not my relations with you, but with other persons.

My dear friend, you needn't have explained at such length what I understand terribly clearly without your help. You, it seems, think you offended me? Nothing of the kind. But you very much offended Aleksin,[94] whom I love, and Malinin,[95] who fell by chance into this mush. I'm sorry about them and feel uncomfortable about it even now. We'll fix it up and discuss it.

Don't worry about Julia,[96] this matter was to her like a blow from a stone to a person about to die. She is very sensitive and clever, and she had everything figured out long ago.

Do you know what tormented me terribly after this incident and why I could not see you until now? It was a feeling of pity and revulsion. If I had seen a woman I loved raped by a seducer and murderer, I might have felt like this, probably. I love you, and not only as a writer colleague—that's not important—I love your restless soul, believe me. You have an immense talent, and a great future. But you are in the power of this dark force, you who can destroy so easily and simply that multitude of forces which holds man's free spirit captive to prejudices—that, brother, is terrible. There's the tragedy!

You call me your older brother. Yes, I am older than you, I have more experience, that's the only reason I'm older. But you have more talent and intelligence. That makes it all the harder for me to see you a helpless captive.

From this cursed illness you've gotten a fear of something, a fear that is incomprehensible to me. I fear nothing and would passionately like to give you my courage; I have it. What can I do, how can I show you the necessity of getting well? I'm lost. But I see that it is possible.

Recently Andreevich came to see me—E. Solov'ë,v[97] you

44

remember, from *Life*. He is a hereditary alcoholic, but this is the third year that he has not drunk and feels no need of it. He was cured by hypnosis. Now there is such a speciality of casting a man into a hypnotic sleep. Listen, try all the poisons, all the acids, fire if necessary, but free yourself from this humiliation, from this weakness of will!

All during this time I have read your book, thought about you, asked about you. And I was hurt that you wrote so little.

Well, good, soon I'll see you. Greetings to your wife and your mother. Warm embraces.

All the best to you, and remember: self-respect first of all!

Aleksei

That's gossip about mysticism. I couldn't say anything to you about the possibility that you might sink into this grey jelly.

43

[*Late* 1902]

Leonid, my gloomy friend, you're a satirist and a most respectable one! Your original fellow[98] has undoubtedly turned out well. The blockheads will be angry. I'm glad.

I'm sending you something, an extremely interesting human document.[99] A splendid illustration of the petty bourgeois psychology. Make use of it. Not at once, not now, but later. Think it over, and—hit him in the snout! By God! I answered him, you know.

Greetings to Deaconess Alexandra[1] and your mother, and your brother the poet, and your brother the artist, and to all the rest of your relatives, for their name is legion.

Well, live! It's interesting to live, really!

Your Aleksei

44

[*Probably Nizhnii Novgorod,* 1902 (?)]

I am sending you two manuscripts: "Night"[2] and a translation from the Ziranian. In my opinion both manuscripts are Ziranian, but they can be published, and should be, if I am not mistaken. "Night" in the beginning recalls Andreev's story "Abyss"[3] but it is a fashionable piece. "A Maiden's Grief" is good, by God.

Skitalets[4] is here. The devil will get you for what you said to me about him! It would be better for me not to tell him about it. First of all, he is as healthy as an ox; second, he isn't drinking and is working hard. Will you come soon? Come! I didn't receive "The Tenor"[5] or more books either. Come! Probably Piatnitskii[6] will be here in a few days.

I warmly press your paw.

A. Peshkov

45

[Late 1902-early 1903 (?)]

And I—along with the public, however offensive this may be! —don't understand the stern justice of the Tenor's[7] death. I don't understand and I don't even want to understand. The tale is a good one, my friend. I have just read it aloud to Skitalets,[8] an artist,[9] my wife, and others. They all praised it, exulted over it, and said: print it! I am also ready to agree with them if you change the ending.

Look: don't have your tenor die, but have his voice fail. This would be more natural and crueler than death. Let him live, but in his empty soul let there be a single dry, corrosive, burning thought: I might have!

I might have sung, I might have seen people on their knees before me, and women kissing my hands. By God! go on in that way!

And sketch in the duke a little more, so that he becomes still better.

And wait to publish it in that form. Now after "Thought"[10] it would not be advantageous for you. Good-bye!

A. Pesh

Please read quickly the manuscript I sent you. And Braliantov,[11] the author of "The Cemetery," is far from a genius, the son of a bitch. He wrote falsely.

46

[*Late* 1902-*early* 1903]

My dear Leonidushka!

Is Christ born?[12] Tell me. How is your wife's health? In case the post is empty, I could be godfather for you. It's all the same to me—I baptize all nations in Orthodox holy water.

S. A. Skirmunt[13] should have sent you the manuscript of "Liberate Life" and "Thought" and Iakubov's[14] story "In the Train." I am also adding his story "On Water and on Land." In my opinion both of them should be published together. If you don't like something, correct it. This Iakubov must be given space, indeed.

Well, good-bye! And say good-bye to your wife. And to your mother, And to your brothers. And if your tongue will stand it, to all the other legions of your blood relatives. Well, friend! with all this soon more children will appear by your hand. Well, never mind! you'll bear it. Each bears life in his own way.

Farewell!

A. Peshkov

You wanted to come here—don't forget.

47

[*Early* 1903 (?)]

My future godchild's father![15]

Skitalets[16] is somewhere in Moscow, so you speak to him yourself about *The Courier*,[17] and so forth.

I'm a bit angry at him, and if he asks why, answer, because of Sorin.[18] And not even because of Sorin, but because of Sorin's bride. And not even because of the bride, but because of the stupidity Skitalets has shown in the matter of Sorin and Co. I am angry too at Arkadii Alekseevskii,[19] since, although he is Arkadii, we are not in Arcadia but in Russia and not Arcadian shepherd boys but writers. The situation is such that the Russian writer must be a political worker now, more than ever.

47

And being such a worker, he cannot and ought not to stack in one woodpile Briusov[20] along with Doroshevich[21] and Asheshov[22] along with Benois.[23] Benois! Well, did Mr. Alekseevskii read his clumsy book about Russian painting?

He, Alekseevskii, asks you, urges you, to give "Mutiny on Shipboard"[24] to their anthology. Give it, if you want to sit in an overshoe. Give it, give it! Along with you in this volume Professor Novgor[odtsev][25] exudes such idealism that he will spoil your artistic sense of smell for ages. And Doroshevich will write something about penal servitude or the ballet. And so forth!

You, friend, go carefully! Everyone wants to put you beside himself, that's very understandable, but don't you allow that. You make up your own mind and put beside yourself whoever you think is worth the honor. The honour is not slight. Especially now, when the audience which used to reject you after "The Foreigner"[26] now gleams like the bright dawn with a very red blush of shame, even on their backs and below their backs, for their stupidity.

Cherish your literary chastity, friend, and don't go into improper establishments. You might offend your wife and the future godfather of your child.

My wife says, by the way, that if the baby is already called Vadim[27] that means you and I must wait for the second for me to be a godfather to a child of yours.

I enclose a letter to your nephew Arkadii Alekseevskii. Send it on when you have read it. I'd send it to him separately, but there's no money for stamps. My friend, how much money I don't have.

Greetings to your wife. And as for the baby, let it yell. When they're young, they're all like that. It will grow up, and it will be quiet, don't worry.

I'm very tired, devil take it.

Good-bye.

My wife will write you something separate.

A. Peshkov

48

[*Late* 1902-*early* 1903 (?)]

My dear Leonid!

I got your letter and felt somewhat guilty about you. I was in Moscow and I didn't come to you, and that's bad since (with one exception) I love you more than anything in Moscow, more than the Cathedral of Basil the Beatified,[28] the Tret'iakovskii Gallery,[29] the Art Theatre, the Rumiantsev Museum,[30] and so on. I love you very much! That's a fact. I'll be in Moscow on the 10th, but I won't see you as I'll have no time and on the 11th I'm going to Penza, but I'll be back on the 15th and I'll stay a week, surely. Then we'll see each other, we'll talk, and all that.

When you find out the day for Fëdor's benefit[31] performance, send my wife and Piatnitskii[32] telegrams and invite them into Box[33] No. 13. Please!

I read about Orël, burst out laughing, and then became sad. But you're a marvel!

Give my greetings to your wife Lexandra. I've no time.

Your A. Pe

49

[*Nizhnii Novgorod* (?), *August* (?), 1903]

My friend!

I have already arranged with Skirmunt[34] about my stay in Moscow, and I'll be staying with him. This is very convenient for me and for you too, believe me. You could get sick of me even if I didn't live with you.

Now: (*a*) Since you're married to a Nizhnii Novgorod woman and have been in Nizhnii several times, you are obliged to take part in a *Nizhnii Novgorod Anthology*, which is being published for the benefit of constructing dormitories for the children of teachers in the city schools. Those participating[35] are all Nizhnii Novgorodites: Minin, Pozharskii,[36] Nikon,[37] Avvakum,[38] Dobroliubov,[39] Kulibin,[40] Speranskii,[41] Pushkin,[42] Boborykin,[43] I, Korolenko,[44] Elpat'evskii,[45] Annenskii,[46] Chirikov,[47] Shatalets,[48] and others.

D   49

(b) Write a one-act play for an art theater. Chirikov, Shatalets, and I are also writing. There will be four acts in all.

(c) Write a good story, without venereal diseases, if it's not too hard for you. Skitalets and Chirikov and I and Chekhov will all do the same. In January a *Literary Volume, No.* 1, published by *Znanie* will appear.[49] Understand? You should be able to understand how this undertaking will benefit us and the public without further explanations. Anyway, we'll speak of it when we meet. But shh! don't let *The Courier* print: "Soon there will be published . . ." Where is "Mutiny"[50]? Are you writing it?

I am writing letters. A disagreeable job.

Greetings to your wife. Mine is dreaming that her daughter has meningitis and is busy buying various cupboards. She has already bought eleven up to now, there are no more in the city. If it should ever come into your head to do her a favor, tell her where she could buy a big second-hand cupboard. Very big. The bigger the better.

Aleksei

50

[*Late* 1903–*early* 1904]

My friend!

The sense of your letter, as I understand it, is this: "V.S. ![51] keep to the old path, this is more to your advantage and more useful to the reader."

It's not convincing. I think that Miroliubov is completely sincere in wavering from side to side; it seems to me that he believes in his own freedom from external influences and supposes that his desire to rise into the sky, even if only to the height of the church bell tower, is a completely free wish.

And under this condition the question of advantage and usefulness is not appropriate.

Let's look at the case: A certain rash man, striving to justify the senseless fact of his personal existence and surveying the chaos in his limp soul, strewn with all sorts of trash, finds among other things in it a small desire: "to serve the people"; with this purpose he opens a pulpit—a journal—and with the help of various persons preaches in his journal the liberation of man from prejudice, premature convictions, authorities, habits. He understands, more or less, that to shake these four pillars on which various cynics have pretended to build palaces of culture and civilization but have actually built larders and cells for the better imprisonment of the free man—he understands, more or less, that this is a respectable and happy task.

But after a little time has passed he feels that this task does not take care of his *personal* doubts, his *personal* fear of life and death, he is not strong or fundamentally honest enough to know how to separate his *personal* desires from the desire common to all men to some extent or another to get free of the cabala of the State, society, religion, instincts, and other superstitions; he is afraid of his own limitations, his own doubts, his solitude. Extending his personal view of life to all, he throws himself fearfully into the corner of a dark larder where a lamp flickers before an ikon to the Mother of God. He screams and bawls: "The harmonious life cannot be constructed without acknowledging an external rational force, without an idea of God. God cannot be comprehended outside those representations of him which the Church has established."

This is called evolution; I call it making philosophy; children, creatures who lie badly, say in such a case: "I wa-a-nt it!" and start wailing.

My friend, I know that the Muse of Philosophy is death and that men philosophize from fear; having granted them this right (why should we embarrass people?) we'll propose to them that they make philosophy with propriety, without taking off their pants in public and without exposing the source of philosophy. We must require a man to do everything beautifully, if possible, and those functions of his organism which cannot be done beautifully let him perform apart, unseen by us.

The Russian writer, in view of the general barbarity of the people surrounding him, must be in part a sanitation officer, sometimes he is obliged to remind the public of the significance of water closets—what can you do? My analogy is coarse, yes, I know, but you can't write anything worse than Russian reality, and my analogy is true.

A motley "greedy youth" is swarming around us, like midges over a swamp. They greedily gobble up fresh and delicious books prepared in the West, and having "glutted themselves" on these books they spoil their stomachs and suffer and throw up and "make philosophy"—I can't approve this. I love the beautiful, I love the bold, I love the free man, but out of respect to him and to myself I demand that he should submit to the requirements of hygiene and sanitation and that the familiar slogan "Strickly forbiden to stop here"[52] should have for him the force of an inner law.

That's my point of view.

Your relationship with Miroliubov is very nice and humane, isn't it? "Blessed is he who caresseth cattle," but for me Mir[oliubov] is a man who, out of a personal desire to restore order in his own soul, publicly "evolutionizes," *i.e.,* corrupts men. He's not alone in doing this, and of course he would not be noticeable if he were alone, but among the evolutionists he is an important figure. A vile time!

By the way: I warn you, it is possible that soon Moscow and Kiev idealists will come to you and invite you to join *New Path*.[53] As you see, I was right when I predicted that all the streams would merge in one current.

A positive journal[54] is also possible, but don't say anything about it for the present to anyone.

Good-bye. Greetings.

This is the second week that the wind has been howling here, damn it!

A. P.

51

[1904 (?)]

Old friend!

You praise me very highly. Watch out, you'll spoil me!

I wrote you about your story,[55] but apparently badly and barely comprehensibly.

Now I have malaria, but it will soon pass away, and I'll go immediately to Nizhnii, and on the tenth I'll be in Yalta, which no one but you and Aleksin[56] should know.

I would like to talk to you about the story before you submit it to *Truth*[57]—but it's all the same; they won't publish it in the summertime.

Leave the story with me, all right? You see, I consider this theme very important, and, what is even more important, very much "yours."

Well?

Best wishes to Skitalets[58] and Sashka Aleksin and your wife and so forth.

A. P.

52

(Telegram)

Nizhnii Novgorod, January 7, 1904

ARRIVING MOSCOW AROUND FIFTEENTH WARM EMBRACES

ALEKSEI

53

[1904 (?)]

The story isn't bad, and Miroliubov[59] is a fool and a boor. In the story there are too many "evil feet—" and your usual repetitions, which transport the reader (like a crab on the end of a tail) into a state of trance. You can of course take them out, but of course you can leave them in too.

I like the story because I see in it one man who has everyone and everything against him. He himself is a blockhead! I'm sorry he didn't know Stoian-Gapkin[60]; there was a man with character and without prejudices!

And therefore we'll publish the story. It would be good, my boy, if you'd submit "Tsar"[61] for the third volume. I'm

submitting "Notes of the Proletariat." I too am composing. And
even poetry. For example:

> A cornet mounted on a whale,
> Riding swiftly through the sky,
> See! his thick-moustached face!
> See! he waves a pistol high!
>> He sticks his foot into his mouth,
>> As he mombles and he sings,
>> But what he sings of—eh, forsooth,
>> No one understands those things!
> Now I don't want you to think this
> Fable mocks some sacred cow,
> But you can read just such nonsense,
> Worse, too, in *New Path*,[62] right now.[63]

This, of course, is very stupid, but even stupider ones could be
written. In these days we learn everything. I can let you in on
some more verses, with a very serious content:

> Long ago there lived a man,
> Comrade was he of truth only;
> Because of truth he was the comrade,
> Though he was known he was not liked.
>> Everybody spoke of him
>> Now with hatred, now with terror,
>> And nowhere was there a shelter
>> For that persecuted man.
> Solitary, strange to all,
> Quietly he died in prison.
> Even then no one would bear
> To the grave this poor man's coffin.
>> We don't know where he was buried,
>> That true friend of tortured justice,
>> My heart only knows that secret,
>> Yes, it knows it, and keeps still!

Verses of a prison supervisor from a story by M. Gorky, written
by the latter in a moment of influenza (not bad verses, by the
way).

Lyric verse is also possible:

> Each morning, opening the shutters,
> I see beneath my window sill
> Swift and straight the streetcar clatters,
> Germans in it, sitting still.
> Oh, if I could be that streetcar,
> Or perhaps a German in there,
> I would fly to other worlds
> From news sheets and from liberals!

In general, verses can be written on various themes and without any sympathy for the reader; that is my profound conviction!

By the way the young writer Tararakhtenberg[64] has portrayed you, Leonid, in his work entitled *Today*, although it was high time to flog him for *Yesterday*. Learn cleverness from me, my friend, and when you learn we'll start working together in one of the Russian humorous journals, which undoubtedly are being published in cemeteries and are not completely soured by the deceased, as is apparent.

You perhaps would like me to write seriously? No! I can't. Now everything serious has become cheap and fly-specked by the liberals. There isn't a single concept, a single idea, which the liberals haven't sat on recently, and all this furniture of the soul is getting sour and has begun to smell horrible.

Good-bye, my deeply respected friend, to hell with you! Etc.

Greetings to A.M.[65] She is a very lively person and understands probably how cheerful it is to live on earth for a man who has three aching teeth which inspire him to write poetry, and who is grabbed by the heels in his sleep by the liberals, and by the collar and all other parts of the organism in the open.

And you, cold criminal, ferocious creature with fire-breathing passions and with an indomitable tendency to debauchery, as Tararakhtenberg described you: see his argument in *Russia* with Kosorotov,[66] who as "Shmel'" also behaves stupidly.

Warm embraces,

A.

55

54

[*Sestroretsk, outside St. Petersburg (?), July–December,* 1904 (?)]
Having read your letters, filled with accounts of all the illnesses
which possess and are destroying you, I began with irritation to
wait for your telegram announcing your death and signed:
"the dear departed Leonid."

But it seems that now you have decided to go to hell and are
going to the Crimea—obviously you think it's best where it's
dullest. Well, what of it? Every writer has his crazy fantasy, and
those writers who don't have fantasy won't be successful.

My sick friend! Write, you devil's snout, some little story for
the *Nizhnii Novgorod Anthology!*[67] Iordanskii[68] has overpowered
me. I have no respite from his pleas! In a letter to Piatnitskii[69]
you state that you are planning to write something—that's good!
But don't forget the third *Znanie* volume, which will be published
to benefit women students in Moscow. Our first two[70] have
gone to the censor, and their fate will be decided in a week.
How it will be decided only the censoring committee knows!

I keep living in the same way. I finished a play.[71] It came out
very dull and flat. Now I have written three bad plays, and you
not a single one yet. A comrade too. Didn't you buy me *The
Scales*,[72] anathema? Well, to hell with you. If you write a story,
show it to me, pray. And farewell!

Japan's[73] a good country, brother! I am reading my second
book about her, a splendid country!

I warmly press your hand and send greetings to your wife.

A.

55

[*July–August,* 1904]
So, my dear Lenia, we buried Anton Chekhov.[74] You know,
I am glad for your sake that you were not at that base ceremony,
which was a triumph of vulgarity. Vulgarity triumphed over the
coffin and grave of her quiet but stubborn enemy, triumphed in
every way, sympathizing but carelessly smiling, triumphed by

shedding corrupt tears and delivering orations. His body was brought in a freight car on which was written in large letters: "For carting fresh oysters," and he was buried in the ground beside the remains "of the widow of a Cossack of the First Petersburg District, Olga Kukoretkina." If you remember, vulgarity was that very gray cloud which he illumined with a uniquely clear although caressing light. In despising he sympathized. My dear friend, the Russian writer is an amazingly solitary, tragically solitary figure, and I warmly press your hand and with all my heart, you devil, I congratulate you on the honor, the tormenting honor, of being one of the best writers of our day. Forgive my lyricism, but that funeral embittered me.

I am all splashed with the graymud of speeches, inscriptions on wreaths, newspaper articles, various conversations. And, chancing to think of my own death, I imagined the ideal funeral to be as follows: a drayman carries my coffin and behind him walks one indifferent policeman. A writer in Russia cannot be buried better, more nobly, more suitably than this. But—details when we see each other; you'll read the papers and feel how everything was done. Look, Leonid: Piatnitskii,[75] Kuprin,[76] and I are undertaking a book in Anton Pavlovich's memory. We think that only Kuprin, Bunin,[77] you, and I will take part in it. Each of us will write something personally about Anton Pavlovich, a meeting with him, some conversation, an impression of his stories, and we'll also submit a story. Kuprin will give his short novel *The Duel*, a long work of about eight signatures. You would contribute splendidly if you would write something like your note on the death of Zola and could also submit "Mutiny on Shipboard" or "The Tsar,"[78] if you have not completely destroyed it and plan to rewrite it. I'll give some story and the article "The Monster," on vulgarity. I'll write Bunin. The volume, of course, will be for sale. We'll set some portion of the income aside for a memorial to Chekhov or some sort of enterprise in his honour. Dear friend, do this! Understand that we need this, need it!

I won't write any more. I feel sick, Leonid, I'm as mean as the devil.

Write me:

> Stara Russa
> Ërzovskaia Street
> c/o Novikov

I am going today. Write quickly. It now seems to *me* that you are offended with me for something; before it was always you who thought this.

Greetings to dear A.[79]

I warmly embrace you,

A.

If you decide to write something personally about Anton Pavlovich, write beautifully, worthily of him. The book must be on sale in September.

56

[*Sestroretsk, outside St. Petersburg* (?), *Autumn,* 1904]

Here it is perfect, I tell you, dear Leonid. For a hundred rubles a month I have a room the size of a riding academy, the ceiling 10 sazhens [70 feet] high, electric lights, a skating rink, skiing, a restaurant, the frozen sea, a pneumatic inhaler, Russian and Roman baths, showers, bathtubs, sprinklers, over the entrance the inscription:

in corpore sano—mens sana

—and no people! Silence. Pines weighted with snow. And the sea, a smooth, even desert, silent and beautiful.

I must find fault with the "inhaler"—I don't know what it is, but obviously something very useful—the inhaler doesn't work. The showers, the tubs, the baths also don't work, they can "exercise an influence" only twice a week, as the man in control of the blessing says. But that's nothing. I know how to cool myself off even without water. The role of Charcot's shower can successfully be replaced by a small dose of scepticism.

No, seriously, it's very nice here. You know—like Devil's Island or St. Helena. Every two hours the train comes from Peter and brings news. I read the telegrams and am poisoned with "patriotism."[80] But this is not dangerous, although it disturbs me. In an alarming and confused time we must depend on precise principles or opinions, the first of which is: The governments are doing the howling, not the people, and they are howling to consolidate their own power, and not in their country's interests. Well, let them howl. Are they beating the people? Of course! They always have, are now, and will beat them until the people learn self-respect. But I'd hang the news-papermen—of course not from the local pine trees. What a rabble! How they lie; what they say! And, taking advantage of a good chance, they are always squaring accounts with us. N. Engelhardt,[81] for example, in the current issue of *New Times* for the 4th, stuck his elbow into you in passing for your story "Original Fellow"[82]—you remember, "And I love Negro women!" In general, Leonid, "our gay days have passed, the time of tears has come"; they'll be zealously baiting us, as you know. But "keep an eye out for the edge and you won't fall over." Write for yourself and spit at everything. Here I sit and I'm writing with satisfaction. The thing will be bad, watery, but never mind. Later I'll pull myself together. You too, my friend, work—and the thing's done. War is a cruel stupidity, and literature is truly the war of a man against society for his own freedom. I am even philosophizing badly. It's because of my foot. My foot, you see, is hurting, and the rascal is hurting so much I can't walk. It hurts amazingly. Rather like a toothache.

My greetings to Vikent'ich,[83] and my very best greetings. He's a good soul and his head is in its place.

With this I remain, on one leg,

Your Aleksei

Greetings to Al. Mikh.[84]

Maybe you'll drop by here? If so, not before the second week of Lent since tomorrow, or rather Friday, I'll be going for about five days to Var. city.[85] And at the end of the first week I'll be in Peter. The trains leave for here every two hours, on the odd hours, and the time of the trip is an hour and fifteen minutes.

Embraces,

A.

57

[*Sestroretsk, outside St. Petersburg*, 1904][86]

Leonid Andreev!

Friendship, combined with boredom, now spurs me to write you another letter. But I don't know what to write you about, since in this frivolous place neither scandals nor events ever occur. Petersburgers arrive, the pancakes are burnt, they revile the Japanese, and they play a wild dance, "The Cake Walk," on the piano. Along the paths, between the pines, three or four ugly faces are walking, and why they are walking here even the devil himself could not make out.

Last night I dreamed that a great monster was riding on me and bawling: "Giddup! I am called the Pneumatic Inhaler, did you know? And I adore riding on writers!" I asked him: "You Sir, are not a publisher or a censor?" "I am one of those extinct monsters in Hutchinson's[87] book but—although I am not literate I can be a censor!" Well, all night he rode me through some strange glades—he said he was a patriot—he and I collected hats to throw at the Japanese.

Then I dreamed that you and I, Leonidka, with the permission of the censor, suddenly married Japanese girls and in a week we had forty pieces of children. When he heard of this marvelous and useful fact, the Japanese emperor himself laughed for three days! And then he placed all of us with our families in the Inhaler and His Majesty ordered us to be blown up into the air.

Well, they blew us up of course, you and I were blown up, and then they sewed us together again—and very inconveniently. They sewed your leg on to me, they also sewed your nose on to me, and attached two extra ears belonging to someone else to my spine. Well, I could spit on that, no one sees me there, but the cursed tailors sewed something . . . where . . . so that I can't sit down! And they sewed someone's finger in place of your nose, if that is a finger and not something else. We should exchange parts, you should sew my leg on to me, I should sew your nose on (so that our dear parts should not spoil en route, they must be packed in snow and covered with carbolic acid).

So, my dear Leonid! You were living peacefully, suddenly along came the Inhaler, and everything has gone to the devil! Very sad. . . . But it would be sadder if suddenly someone else's leg began to hurt as if it was one's own.

I, brother, was an honorary member of the sanatorium in Alupka, the president of which is the surgeon Bobrov, but the government ordered that I be expelled. They expelled me. I'm not crying. I don't lose much, but I remain without an honor and Surgeon Bobrov without a member.

So, a former academician,[88] soon to be a former member—everything passes in this world, only my debts grow bigger. But I won't pay them, I haven't the means, and that's far from a joke, and besides, I have no time. In the afternoon now I write plays, tales, and short stories, at night I catch fleas in bed—well, when do I have time to pay debts?

But I understand, however, that I should long ago have finished this short but serious letter. Well, farewell! live sensibly. Don't doze off in the daytime. Stay well.

I remain myself, former member and academician, now, only hooligan,

A. Pesh.

I was in Petersburg today, got your letters there. They were very pleasant for me. But you should write me here! My address is simple and clear: Petersburg Guberniia, Sestroretsk Health Resort. That's all.

You tell your wife that I would send her a self-portrait, it would flatter me very much, but I have no portraits. I only see myself in the mirror—it is the only one I have and a bad one, but if she wishes I'll send it to her so that she may admire me! I'll be very glad to. That's a fact.

Farewell!

My name day is on March 17.

Give me a revolver.

Listen, friend! It's a long time before my name day, but do this for me: subscribe in I. P. Piatnitskii's[89] name to the journal *The Scales.*[90] And I will be grateful to you until the end of the

Russo-Japanese conflict caused by the Manchurian-Korean adventure.[91] Do it! And one can't survive only on serious books. The devils! Why don't you send me the Chekhov material?[92] Lazybones!

Viktor Mirov[93] is swearing. Such a wordy idiot!

A.

58

[Late October-early November, 1904]

Dear friend!

I have joined *Our Life*[94]. There has been a split among the liberals: the rights, the fathers, have split off from the lefts, the children. The rights have *Son of the Fatherland* and a "dock-tailed" constitution. The lefts have *Our Life* and a democratic constitution. The rights, it seems, have already entered into some sort of agreement with the government and have probably sold something. Something or someone, for example, "the enemy from within."

Friend, I want you to take part in this *Our Life* either as James Lynch[95] or Andreev—as you wish. I've gotten some money, the first issue should come out on the 4th. Tell Evgenii[96] that I want him too, very much. I know that he has been written to about this—as you have—but now it has become clear: the newspaper should be bold and honest, we must make it vivid and talented. If you, Evgenii, or Gavrilych[97] can give us something for the 4th, it would be superb! I'll try. I have no time to write in detail, I am now going [to] Riga. Greetings. I'll be in Petersburg on the 2nd.

I press your hand.

Your Al . . .

59

[St. Petersburg (?), late 1904-early 1905[98]]

My deep-red Markobrunner!

I got a letter, but I didn't get the story.[99] Will I? I am glad for you, glad in advance, since I am sure that it's good. I can already see from your letter that it is good, and from your attitude toward the devil I can feel: it is good! Hurry all the evil spirits of *Znanie*, hurry those draymen! Nothing has come yet from Bunin,[1] and I don't know where he is. But that doesn't hold us back.

As soon as you send your "Beautiful [Red] Laugh" we will give it to the printer immediately, don't worry! And it will fit in very harmoniously: you are describing war, Kuprin[2] the warriors—Banzai! Kuprin's memoirs are published, *The Summer Folk*[3] also will soon be ready, you have hurried just in time, and Bunin and Shatalets[4] will come after you—and the volume will be ready! We have more material than necessary for one book, and it is possible that we will put out two more. Write! Write, friend.

And I'm not mad at all; on the contrary, I feel splendid; I hate everyone with a gay, stormy hatred, and—I tell you sincerely!—the day of the first presentation of *The Summer Folk*[5] was the best day of the improbably long, interesting, and good life which I have made for myself. My dear soul, how wonderful I felt when after the third act I went right up to the footlights, stood and looked at the audience, simply looked, not bowing to it, and an immense hot joy burned in me; I would like you to feel this inexpressible, indescribable pleasure, this human pride, this strength: to hell with it! Wonderful! Banzai!

Banzai, Leonid! They hissed when I wasn't there, and no one dared hiss when I came out—cowards and slaves they are! Their names are Merezhkovskii, Filosofov, Diaghilev,[6] etc., they consider themselves free people, and they haven't strength to stand nose to nose with those they hate—is that freedom? Is freedom possible without manliness? Without force? To hell with men without force and manliness!

I strongly recommend to you the articles in the *Petersburg Herald* and the *World*, an interview with Merezhkovskii in the *Petersburg Gazette*,[7] and the poem "The Liberal" in *Russia*;[8] the last has no relation to *The Summer Folk*, but it is interesting for itself.

The *feuilleton* you sent to *Our Life*[9] is about two years late, and, after consulting with Nevedomskii,[10] who sincerely likes you, we decided not to publish it. Here it is pleasant. The weather is terrible, I am coughing blood, Mar'ia Fëdorovna[11] is in the hospital and has just had an operation, but that is all bearable, even not noticeable, since that isn't what's important, my friend. We will all die, but you and I will never entirely die, that's what's important!

During *The Summer Folk*, the public, I am told, berated me roundly. Potapenko,[12] it seems, cursed the newcomers to their faces, someone shouted at them "vulgar!"—in general the petty bourgeois were remorselessly attacked, and I thrashed them! For the first time I thrashed them—understand, for the first time I *felt* that I had thrashed them.

No, life is good, I love life! I love you with a warm love, deeply and sincerely, I love my noble Marusia,[13] my beautiful friend and wife, I love Konstantin Piatnitskii,[14] who is by nature as steady as a knight's castle. In his strong body there is a splendid soul, a soul burning always peacefully and evenly, like a solitary bonfire in the deserted steppe on a quiet summer night. I love all the rest too, and even those who are repulsive to me; it seems to me I love them a little too because—they make me feel myself!

How important it is, how glorious it is—to feel oneself!

Of course *The Summer Folk* did not rise in my estimation after all this. *The Summer Folk* is not art, but it is clearly a well-aimed shaft and I am glad, like a devil who has tempted the righteous to get shamefully drunk.

Well, enough! On the 21st I will give a reading here for charitable purposes. The purpose is good. Will you come? Will you come tomorrow? All right? Telegraph if you agree. You'll stay with us at 20 Znamenskaia. Embraces, kisses, greetings.

Miklashevskii[15] came.

A. . .

60

[St. Petersburg (?), late 1904–early 1905]

To my mind you are right, friend, excerpt fifteen[16] should be thrown out; it doesn't strengthen the impression, it waters the blood with muddy water, and even the style is not appropriate, from the literary point of view. And from the social viewpoint, it strengthens the position of those who will curse the story. They will of course take the point of view that the hero of the story is psychically abnormal, this is inevitable! I even foresee in the future an article headed: "War in the Mind of a Madman." We must not put such a weapon in the hands of the "patriots" and chauvinists, you understand?

We must also throw out excerpt seven, since it will inevitably be used against the Japanese; it will be used as a demonstration of their atrocities.

It seems to me that the newspaper clipping, which I have pasted to the top of this letter, makes your point more sharply and clearly than excerpt 15 does. Just think—children! Please, Lenka, discard the seventh and fifteenth! Really, the story will gain strength from this.

In the middle of the story there is something psychologically impossible and impermissible: which of the brothers wrote the scene in the bathtub? The first. You think this is possible in this form? You must make absolutely clear up to which point the first brother is writing the journal. He is writing it only until he reaches home. Otherwise, I don't see how the second brother could write the way he did. Make this change, it's easy.

I don't like the ending. It's not terrifying. When the general battle began, it was good, but after the return home—no, it's no good! The earth, vomiting forth bodies from its entrails—it didn't come off. Ezekiel describes this more beautifully and more terribly. You must stop somewhere earlier.

In general, I think the story is extraordinarily important, timely, forceful—all that is so—but to make a strong impression it must be made healthy. The facts are more terrible and more significant than your attitude toward them in this case. The first half is very good, very, but you must discard the doctor standing on his head. It is ridiculous. It is a stupid ugly mug at Chekhov's funeral, it is the sound of a workman's accordion in the midst of Beethoven's requiem. It is ridiculous and disturbing.

On the thirteenth page, "searching," "shuddering," "scratching themselves," "striving," "strange" are all crowded in one sentence and deafen it with hissing.

"There are many insane. More than wounded." Page 20. Isn't it abrupt, in so categorical a form? It seems to me that the reader should feel that there are a lot of them and that it should not be announced baldly.

On page 53—"They are still *weeping* because of the war, and they themselves are *weeping*, what is the *meaning?*" A terrible rhyme.

On page 56—"Each of them was silent," and then immediately "they coughed, blew their noses. . . ."

On page 82—"triangular heads between the neck and the chin," I can't visualize this, what is it?

Don't get angry with me, Leonid, I so much want your story to make the most overwhelming possible impression, and I don't want them to nag at you for trifles!

I embrace you warmly; greetings to A.M.

Your Alek. . .

I am very tired of this place, but I'll drag along until the 22nd.

I have read the story twice; I read it through when I got it and just now. It has a very strong effect, that's true!

[The following clipping from a newspaper is pasted to the first page of the letter.]

A children's game. In the district near Cheliabinsk, according to the *Samara Gazette,* the following terrible event took place:

Some youngsters had decided to play "war"; they divided up and formed two camps: "the Russians" and "the Japanese." Finally "the Russians" won and the leader of the "Japanese," "Kuroki," was taken captive. . . . Passions ran strong. . . .

"What will we do with the prisoner?" they asked; they held a "council of war" and immediately passed a resolution:

"Kuroki is to be hanged!"

A rope was found, soon a gallows was set up. . . .

This "game," to tell the truth, had a terrible end: a death rattle was heard in the throat of the boy who had played the part of "Kuroki." He had fallen into the noose. The boys became frightened and ran away, and at that very instant the unfortunate child died. . . .

61

[*Late 1904-early* 1905 (?)]

My friend!

Did you keep the rough draft?[17] Have two more copies made of it directly or bring it here, we'll submit it here. If you don't do this, we shall have to send to the press the copy which you sent us, and that means that when you come we won't have the story. We need three copies, one for the printer's, another for abroad,[18] and a third to have at home to check the proofs. Don't fail to do this!

Then—please hurry Bunin,[19] hurry him with all your might.

What of Serafimych?[20] The rest[21] will wait until we see each other.

Aleksei

62

[*St. Petersburg, about February* 14, 1905]

My friend!

It now appears that there will be two volumes. In the volume in honor of Chekhov[22] there will be a very nice article by Kuprin,[23] *The Summer Folk*,[24] a new play by Naidenov,[25] Stepan's[26] verses; we'll ask Bunin[27] for some poems, probably he'll send a story, and—K.P.[28] says that he, that is Bunin, has written reminiscences of Anton Pavlovich. We need your story. The second volume will have a long story by Kuprin, a play by Chirikov,[29] a very interesting story by Gusev,[30] and two short ones by me. We need your story.

I am counting on you, my stiff-horned angel. Write. I'll explain in detail when I see you, since I'll get to Moscow anyway on the 20th.

Then you submit some sort of story or two from those

published in *The Courier* ("The Gendarme," "The Marseillaise," "The Little Negro")[31] for the Nizhnii Novgorod teacher's volume![32] Please, please, even I am tired of asking.

Tomorrow I am going to Riga,[33] a magnificent city! Amazingly beautiful, clean, interesting. I'll spend two or three days there.

Then I'll go, then I'll come, I'll drop in, and I'll leave. That's a fact.

My Riga tonic: Pervaia vygonnaia damba, House 2, Apartment 5. Extraordinarily pleasant.

I press your hand.

Aleksei

63

[Riga (?), before February 4, 1905]

I want to yell at you, my fine friend—my tongue is itching and even whitening from a malicious desire to say to you straight at your fat stomach: "Intellectual!" But I love you, I respect you, I'm sorry for you, and anyway I know that you haven't deserved this shameful epithet.

I read your letter to M.F.,[34] because when she had read it she burst into tears and ordered the trunks brought so she could go to Moscow to kill Serëzha[35] and Trepov.[36] I told her that of course it would be stupid and wild not to kill them, but why throw trunks around? Yes, so I too read your letter[37] and was upset.

Why are you moaning, why are you groaning? They've beaten up the public? The public in general must be beaten as long as it permits it, it is essential to beat the public, since it must be taught to fight, this is so obvious, this is so simple, and believe me this is my sincere conviction. Now think calmly and simply: each individual making up the public, man or woman, it's all the same, is an autocrat in respect to his own wife or husband and even more in his relations with his property, his houses, skirts, watches, beds, breeches, chairs, neckties, and other objects of primary importance. If you take away from this man his own living inventory, (*i.e.*, his husband or wife) or his weapons of production (*i.e.*, his chair or bed) he, regardless of

his chickenish temperament, will protest, cry out, even appeal
—in brief, will defend himself. He always defends himself
comically and pitifully, but in this case it is the effort to defend
himself, not the form of the defense, which matters.

Now: let's take an autocrat, a man like the tsar, having substantial property and a bunch of servants made up of simple
lackeys, but of lackeys endowed with unlimited power. The
public comes out in the streets and shouts at him: "Give us half
your power, give it up! Go to the devil! Down with your order!
To the hogs down on the farm with you, and all your tribe!"

Leonid—let's be just! These popular sayings are offensive!
They are upsetting! Imagine that you are Leonid the First, your
ancestors have sat tranquilly on Russia's back for 292 years, and
suddenly the public comes out on the street and bawls at you:
"Get out!"

My friend, the habit of autocracy is a very deeply ingrained
habit and—I assure you!—you also would immediately send
against the public all your janitors, cooks, uncles, and all the rest
of the mob with orders to heat them up, and you yourself would
stand behind the window frames and joyfully watch your
myrmidons beat up the mugs of the crowds, you'd be extremely
pleased. The conclusion: don't blame the tsar for beating up the
people; it is so natural and understandable in his position! But
discard sentimentalism and all human feelings, which are completely superfluous under autocracy, even harmful, put all this
aside and look at the public with simple, clear eyes: how idiotic
it is!

My friend! What would you say of a man who plans to forge
red-hot iron with his bare fist? Or of Kuropatkin,[38] if he forced
soldiers to fight against the Japanese with their teeth alone, not using
any artillery? You would respond negatively to these characters.

Man loves freedom . . . rather, someone imagines that he needs
freedom for the better arrangement of his affairs, that it is essential
for rational reasons, or for the beauty of life, or that it is necessary
ideologically. What would this man sacrifice personally for the
triumph of freedom? If he would give his life to establish freedom, that's one thing, but if he would only give a black eye or

two broken teeth, he won't set up freedom, and neither his broken teeth nor his black eyes will raise my respect for him; that is also a fact.

And don't fall into hypochondria, my friend, it's not worth it! Two hundred black eyes will not deck Russian history in a brighter color; for that you need blood, and lots of blood, as blood is the only decorative material that is really lasting and that will deck events in a gay red color.

And so—don't weep, my child, don't weep in vain! Everything goes on as it should, and completely properly. Life is built on cruelty, horror, force; for reconstruction a cold, rational cruelty is necessary, that's all. They are being killed? They must be killed. Otherwise what will you do? Go to Count Leo Tolstoy and wait with him for the wild beasts to become senile and the slaves, their legal food, to be eaten up?[39] This is a very long and dull story, and it is somehow shameful for a man to be taken up with it.

Good-bye!

I philosophized like a factory chimney, black and smoky, but truly, it's my deep conviction that no other philosophy is fitting, and also not very clever, moderately speaking.

M.F. greets you and A.M. Tell Gavrilych[40] to send his story to Petersburg. I'll be there the 17th.

Trepov and Serëzha must be killed. Simply come and shoot them. All right? Well, I embrace you, friend.

A.

64

(Telegram)

Riga, [early 1905 (?)]

MAN WHO KNOCKS ON ALL CLOSED DOORS SUPERB FULLY INDEPENDENT THEME[41] YOU ROB SELF BY INSERTING PHANTOMS IN THEME URGENTLY REQUEST REMOVAL STORY WON'T LOSE VERY SIMPLE AND GOOD OUR FRIENDLY OPINION WRITING THANKS

MAR'IA[42] ALEKSEI

70

65

Dear Sir!

My dear friend!

In returning enclosed the historic document,[43] with sorrow I must state that even at the moment of its birth it obviously had all the signs of old age, of canine old age, so to speak. At that very moment it aged completely, and it even smells like a corpse. I can't sign it, of course; it's not a promissory note, but I have decided not to show it around since I'm ashamed. And even afraid: now the public is in such a wild mood that after reading such a document it may inflict "sore wounds and even mutilations." In conclusion I say, take my modest advice: light a fire, put this document into the flames, and it will be a fully noble end for a noble passion; if you don't, I fear, this paper will be utilized by evil persons for external use in some intimate, although natural, circumstances.

To console you and all who signed this stirring proclamation along with you, I'll say that messieurs the littérateurs of the city of Petersburg wrote just as badly, although more opportunely.

Port Arthur[44] has fallen; *Our Life* says on this subject that it "will not throw stones at Stössel," and it seems to me that so noble a promise is not completely clever.

Up to fifty per cent of those signing all possible declarations are Jews, which also is not entirely tactful on the part of messieurs, the Russian liberals, since this fact will give shrewd people the right to say that in Russia only Jews are demanding a constitution and other things, it will permit anti-Semitism to flourish, and will magnify its growth.

Tell this to those chatterers who themselves apparently can't guess what they are playing with by permitting such a *fact*.

Also say that it is time to change from a spontaneous movement to an organized one, that all social groups must be attracted into the process of remaking life, that for example salesmen, petty officials in various private organizations, and others are still not under the influence of the progressive segment of society, and that if this segment cannot organize them the police will.

Also, think: in propagandizing for peace, aren't messieurs the liberals leaving their leader, Marshal Oyama, idle, and thus are they not cutting the knots on which they are depending?

Keep in mind: it is possible that "Red Laugh"[45] will be cut out, and therefore, to prevent the Chekhov volume from coming out without you, send us "Tsar"[46] immediately. The volume went to the censor today—we purposely held it until the last day since over the holidays the censors, we hope, will be drunk, and when drunk a man is more freedom-loving. This is called: fine calculation.

Good-bye! I'm as busy as Satan and tired as Stessel'.

And shouldn't we start protesting against Ivan the Terrible? Think how many people he thrashed! . . .

I'm angry, a bit. Therefore, I see an awful lot of people.

My respects to Alexandra Mikhailovna.[47] Tell her not to give you ink when the impulse comes over you to sign Moscow protests, since it would be more fitting to sign them in Gol'tsev's[48] spittle.

Don't be angry with me, my dear friend, I'm not worth getting mad at! Read Artsybashev's[49] story in *Journal for All* and see what a true man, a positive type, should be. Even a hungry bear wouldn't eat such a man, so repulsively sweet, a sugar beet and not a man!

Too bad I wasn't in the heroine's place, I'd have raped him! And then, after taking off his panties, I'd give him a long beating with a twig broom on his buttocks and would keep saying: don't be a positive type, don't, don't, you son of a bitch! And then, taking him under the arms I would honorably drown him in the sink.

And then I'd say to Artsybashev and Miroliubov that they both are . . . positive types, too.

No, tell me, can you imagine a country where a writer could present Ivan Landé to the public as a positive type?

A lot is needed for that; the people of such a country would have to have renounced human rights over the course of centuries and the feeling of self-respect would have to have completely died out in them.

I am writing you a lot, just like a nun to her lover on the eve
of Lent.

Farewell.

Something is hurting me, either my foot or my tooth, I have
no time to find out which precisely.

Sometime I'll come to Moscow.

A.

Look up the text of *The Marseillaise* in Lamartine's *History of
the Girondists*, a book which is hard to find. Simpler, write for
Dumas's *La Comtesse Charny*, Suvorin publishers.

66

[*Yalta*,[50] *March* 29–May 7, 1905]

Both intelligence and stupidity in overabundance are repulsive,
friend; you are as right as Adonai, who considered the Jews the
best of people.

Too much money, glory, intelligence, and stupidity, any kind
of superfluity, my decrepit friend, creates slavery, a chain, but
each baron has his fantasy, and let people brag out of superfluous
vulgarity, it's only useful for you and me, as we see it.

From the above you may see that Yalta is already affecting me;
my brains are crushed and confused by the wind; inside is the
roar of the sea waves—it's not because my stomach is out of order
but because of the weather, the cruel weather!

I came here, I don't know what for, and I sit. I tried to write
about Chekhov, but it seems this is not my specialty. I can't
write about the dead. And I should write about Chekhov the
writer long, in detail, painstakingly, and there's no time for that.

Too bad about Skitalets,[51] and perhaps it isn't too bad, simply
unpleasant. I don't like intemperate men, and although I too
have bad teeth I don't like anything infirm. You, my mountain
angel, should go to S. Morozov[52] and advise him to buy *The
Courier.* I have already spoken to him about it, but in passing, not
thoroughly. You talk it over. The plan still stands. The editors
will be Asheshov,[53] Chirikov,[54] you, I, and some other such

archangels. The paper might turn out gay, even if short-lived. You can talk with Savva [Morozov] simply, clearly, very conveniently.

M.F.'s[55] address:

Riga, Russian Theatre.

If you send her your photograph, she will be pleased, since she has tremendous respect for you, and this is as much a fact as that Orlenev[56] is approaching me on the staircase. How do you do! . . . And you, m'sieur, au revoir!

Write! Write well. Write very well. And you'll write splendidly, so that this same reader may bite his own nose from sincere amazement before you, my dear Señor!

Greetings.

I kiss you on your luxurious beard. . . . Is it red? Or light blue? I forgot! This is natural, since I saw it with my naked eye, not under a microscope, as I should have.

Well, good.

"Ghosts" are sitting beside me and smell of burnt vodka.

67

[*Moscow (?), August, 1905*[57]]

Dear Leonid!

I decided not to drop in on you, under the mistaken impression that some people who had just arrived were waiting for me at Mustomiaki.[58] It turned out that these people were not due to come until the evening.

It was very annoying, as it would have been more convenient and easier to tell you about the situation personally. This is it: the questionnaires[59] have been composed, D. N. Ovsianiko-Kulikovskii[60] and Vinaver[61] are editing them, and they'll be ready for the Press in a couple of days.

But we must add to the list of questions directions to the interviewers. These directions should be written by us: you, me, Sologub.[62] I enclose my draft. You write yours, and then send both sheets to F. K. Sologub. That's the arrangement. Don't send it by post, it will get lost.

I'll be in Peter on the 20th, and you'll probably be there then? A meeting has been called at Vinaver's on the 21st on the question of organizing the Russian League of Philosemites. It would be good if I could talk with you before the 20th—wouldn't you agree to come to Mustomiaki? Please! I've caught bronchitis, and also I'm expecting guests.

Best wishes, and my best to your wife.

Send an answer with the cabman.

A. Pesh

68

[*St. Petersburg or Finland, August-September,* 1905]

Dear Leonid!

It was decided that on the 27th (*i.e.,* today) you and I would meet at F. K. Sologub's[63] and compose the test of the directions.

But I have come down with bronchitis, and for four or five days I won't be able to go out in the street.

In the interval I'll write a draft of the directions. I'll ask you to do the same—please! I telegraphed Sologub that I won't be coming; perhaps you might telegraph him so he won't be offended?

Giurdzhan, the sculptor, who is bringing you this letter, would like to make a bust of you. He's a talented man and a wonderful fellow. He studied in Paris and is very well known there.

Good luck, my greetings to your family.

Best wishes,
A. Peshkov

69

[*Autumn,* 1905]

My dear Leonid!

It seems to me that Fëdor Kuz'mich's[64] directions are written convincingly enough and that we both, you and I, may sign them, so you won't have to compose any others.

Are our three signatures enough, or need we add to our names those of Arsen'ev,[65] Ovsianiko-Kulikovskii,[66] Miakotin,[67] etc?

This question isn't clear to me.

Then: the directions don't have an ending, that is, there's no invitation to the interviewers to express themselves. But that can be done in two words.

I must have a talk with you, and I can't come to see you before the 2nd or the 3rd—will you be at home? If I came on the 3rd, on the 4th we might travel to Petersburg together, all right? Good luck!

I am writing a proclamation and I'll bring it to you. You also please try to write a manifesto in accordance with our discussion at Ketcher's.[68]

All the best!
A. Pesh

70

[1905 (?)]

My dear Leonid!

I didn't like your story.[69] It is written in an excessively "studied" way; there are a lot of superfluous words, which tarnish it with boredom and weigh it down and spoil its inner beauty, the beauty of its meaning. Its meaning is deep and important, much more so than you apparently think. And it must be vigorously cleaned, cut, polished, like a diamond.

And look: your Babylonian superman is not very arrogant; there is still not much which is truly human in the fact that he dared to eat warmish shit; this is only "too human," or, in other words, swinish, zoological. Any man can rouse the wild beast or the cattle instinct in himself, but to raise oneself on the wings of pride and longing to the gods, to the heavens, and to hurl a few questions into the face of the gods—that would be a good trick! You seem to want to justify the cattle—well, is it worth it? All are busy doing that, my friend.

But, more simply, in my opinion you should have made the tsar's *experience of the depth of human slavery* the theme of your story; this you did not completely succeed in doing, Leonid. You paid too much attention to the tsar and lost sight of the slaves. And surely at the present time we Russian writers should not be inspiring our readers with the longing to be tsar—what use is that to them!—but with revulsion against slavery.

My friend, you should pay more attention to the slaves and give them more space. The tsar becomes bored not because he is seeking equality with the gods and loses faith in their existence —that's all right if you want it—but because on earth there are slaves everywhere and he, among them, is solitary on earth. Do you understand me? And of course you're not offended? Don't be offended.

After Father Vasilii,[70] the story, in the form which I have it, is weak. And as I said it is too "studied." Such a theme should be written in the language of the Flaubert legends. My dear friend, don't hurry with this, I beg you! Don't give it to *Truth*[71] before autumn, and rewrite it over the summer.

Well, I've written a play. It came out watery, flat, garrulous and ordinary—very vile! But I'm not losing heart! I'm beginning a second. And if you'll let me have the theme of the "Astronomer"[72] I'll write a third. Will you? It's coming out very nicely: the astronomer, a teacher, a veterinarian. The astronomer's wife, the teacher's sister, the veterinarian's mother. A blacksmith, who is to kill the astronomer, a holy pilgrim, a gay house-painter who is a skeptic, a merchant who wants order and harmony, and—THE CROWD. Will you let me have it?

I'll be grateful, etc.

I'm going to Nizhnii at the end of the month, then down the Volga and through the Caucasus to Yalta. Will I run into you? I hope so!

Greetings. To everybody.

And rewrite "The Tsar"—please do!

I embrace you, I crush your ribs, I kiss you, etc. Long live Japan![73]

Write me, c/o *Znanie*.

" Death to flies!"

That's what I have called my comedy. What will I do with your story?

A. Pesh

71

My friend!

This is the problem: there are various kinds of livestock; the bull is livestock, and the lion and the pig are livestock, but neither with a telescope nor with a microscope can I see in a pig "its own beauty and meaning." You have actually written an apology for swinish livestock in your letter. That's not important. And in the conduct of a hog there can never be "more pride and freedom than in heroism," that is a fact! Pride is beautiful, freedom too, freedom may be terribly beautiful, but pigs and freedom are incompatible, just as pride and pigs are incompatible. And you have turned your tsar precisely into a hog. This is not beautiful, although perhaps justified, and it does not relate to the theme of your story—understand![74]

"To affirm one's 'Ego' on one's own ruins"—this is cleverly put, but again you must remember this: this has been done, and very often, by very many people. This was done when man conquered the cattle instinct in himself and on its corpse was himself burnt up in the spirit of freedom. Don't forget that in a man the cattle instinct is stronger than the man and that this fact is obvious and needs no apology. Don't forget also that there is a great difference between cattle and wild beasts.

You "need the image of a solitary, free, and bold man who would reject wisdom, power, and glory in the name of something better"—you must hunt for this better thing in some other place, not in the transformation into swine. It's simply offensive to listen to you!

You see, man stands between two bottomless gulfs, birth and death. He has imagined how the universe was constructed and knows that the earth one fine day may fall into the sun and turn into steam, along with him, libraries, museums, babies, valuables —along with all the material and spiritual work of many centuries, along with everything dear to him, that he loves. Now look at him from this tragic aspect, as Ecclesiastes once tried to do, and then look again: then you'll see that, although he knows of the future ruin, ruin without a trace, of all the work of his muscles and his spirit, he keeps on working, keeps on creating, and not to create in order to put off this ruin without a trace but simply from some sort of proud stubbornness.

"Yes, I'll perish, and perish without a trace, but first I'll build temples, and I'll create great works. Yes, I know that they too will perish without a trace, but I'll create them just the same, since I want to!"

That's the human voice. And believe me, the real man, who is truly free, always values his human worth, and he is always courageously conscious of the mortality both of himself and of all that surrounds him.

All this is confused, forgive me! There's so little time. I enclose your story. I just came here today from Nizhnii. Ekaterina Pavlovna[75] will be here the day after tomorrow on her trip abroad.

Well, all right, write "The Astronomer."[76] I also will write one. I won't publish it or stage it, but I'll write it. Then I'll read it to you.

Greetings. I won't get to Iasli.[77] Good-bye. Write me, c/o *Znanie.*

A. P. . .

Old fellow, do give us a story for the *Nizhnii Novgorod Anthology!*[78] I beg you! They are overwhelming me! Write something Crimean Sea-ish or mountain-ish.

And Skitalets's[79] wife remains unseen? That's strange. Is he himself to be seen?

Write.

Your A. . .

72

[1905 (?)]

Here's the story, my friend:

Along with the books for K.P.,[80] we must send cover portraits of the authors. And therefore, get and send me here, as soon as possible, pictures of you, of Teleshov,[81] of Serafimovich,[82] of

Chirikov,[83] of Bunin,[84] of Skitalets,[85] of Elpatii,[86] of Garin[87] (his wife lives in Moscow, get it from her, and although he's got lost now he himself will probably turn up!). Elpatii also will be in Moscow in a few days. Belousov's[88] isn't necessary? or is it? Do this quickly! Bogdan[89] should have given you my note. Write! quicker! better! more!

A.

Give Ivan Bunin 5 rubles for me, and—when I am summoned before the terrible court of the Lord, I promise you I'll arrive at the session in a dress coat and white tie! Could more be asked of me for 5 silver rubles?

I conjure you by all the devils—hurry Skitalets, Bunin, Serafimovich, Teleshov. And—shame on you! you object: why has the plan been changed? But you give your stories to Kozhedralkin![90]

And so forth. I feel that there is no logic in this. But there is deep feeling!

A.

73

[St. Petersburg (?), not later than early December, 1905]

My dear humorist!

This is the third day I have been living here and occupying myself with observations of the liberals, trying to clarify to myself where, precisely, the liberal ends and where the senior janitor begins. And why, when he often pronounces the word "constitution" (*konstitutsia*) it begins to sound like "penitentiary" (*kutuzka*)? And why, when he talks of subjects dangerous for his health and convenience he says "we," but when he is talking of less dangerous things he says "I"? All this and much more has my full attention as a tranquil and peace-loving observer of human customs.

And by the way our plan to bring K.P.[91] books and portraits is a poor and superfluous project. He has an overabundance of books and almost all our pictures. We must think of something more elegant and not so original as pictures. Even little recruits going to war give pictures to their father-commanders, but recently with my own eyes I saw a battery crew brought before a commander, and in the group one soldier obviously thumbed his nose at him; all the others could not conceal their joy at the parting, and it even shone in their buttons.

Think, dear colleague of the pen, how should we do this? I can't think. I can scold, but I can't think! Since I don't want to be like a liberal, who only ponders on how to betray his motherland most cleverly to those who want to buy it. If the word "betray" offends you, I can replace it with another: "sell." I am amenable and modest.

Further. Be good, o thou impartial priest of anti-Christ; press Shatalets[92] to send his poems and story immediately. Please do the same with Teleshov,[93] Serafimovich,[94] and Leonid Andreev. Urge this last particularly strongly since he is an incorrigible dawdler! And tell Bunin[95]—what about him? Hey, gentlemen, young men! Hurry to live, or you'll get old. . . .

It has just struck two, so it must be now already the 6th.[96] In a few hours the well-meaning Russian people will begin to make history or a scandal. I think history (and probably sordid) will be made under a roof and scandal on the street, and besides, the scandal will be history and the history a scandal.

Alexandra Mikhailovna[97] wrote about Alekseevskii.[98] He spoke. They listened—without pleasure. There were two crocodiles sitting in each section, and all such, as you know, are fierce. They talk in an unknown language, in which Russian words sometimes chance to appear, but this does not make it comprehensible to me. They are all as serious as bricks. They promised . . . Tell Alexandra Mikhailovna that this is a hopeless project and that Alekseevskii will sooner become boss in paradise than in Our Life,[99] which, probably, soon will not be ours. Now everything is happening fast. Russian life today is like the horse belonging to cabby No. 9027, who, having kicked over the shafts, galloped, galloped, and by herself, without need, galloped into her paddock. I saw her. And it seemed to me, from her eyes, that even if she had completely broken the shaft and had thrown off her collar, she would even then have galloped into her paddock. So delicate is her education, so tender her heritage. You think I am a pessimist? I am not at all a pessimist, but I'm simply —sleepy.

By the way, about paddocks: the Russian petty bourgeois—a good petty bourgeois, of course—loves his paddock! Yesterday Naidenov[1] sent me an angry letter with a letter from Nemirovich[2] enclosed. Naidenov is swearing; he is cursing the Art Theatre.

Nemirovich's letter to Naidenov begins thus: "Dear S. A.! I have thought up a fourth act for *Avdotia's Life*." Fine!? And he has really thought up something bittersweet, limp, impotent. Naidenov says, "But that's unseemly." Nemirovich's letter is stupid and insolent. This gentleman imagines himself to be a literary district supervisor, no less. What sort? *Mania grandiosa,* in full display form.

Dear Leonid! I have a tremendous plan—and practical. Write a play. Write two plays. Write five. When I see you I'll explain what's up, and meanwhile silence, like a real corpse.

Oh my friend! How I would like to see the liberals as corpses! This would be the most suitable and quietest party—forgive me for the pun, there are things even heavier than that: for example, the sideboard which K.P. has bought.

Did you get my inspired letter[3] from Riga about the man who knocks on all closed doors? What an immense man, Leonid, how bold! What have you decided? And why didn't you telegraph?

I press your hands. Greetings to your family.

A. . .

74

[1905]

If you want to get hold of *The Girondists*[4] you'll have to ask the booksellers.

I can't send the story to you since it is being published from the draft. You wrote K.P.[5] that you wanted to get marks[6] from the Germans for "Laugh"—but, my friend, it's too late! You should have thought of it earlier—and before you said to hell with them, those Germans! If we begin this delay now, we'll have to hold the volume at least a month, and we have already held it enough.

Tell me, when is the concert Alexandra Mikhailovna[7] wrote about? As you know, I am lecturing on the 15th in Riga, on the 22nd and 23rd in Peterburg.

But you write—don't get angry!

I am glad that Nemirovich[8] failed at the monastery. He must get out of the theater and go to hell—then there'd be two of us. You know how good this would be? Two! And an e-normous troupe! And an exclusively literary repertoire!

Crocodiles and scorpions!

Shakee handee. Oyama. Nosovato.[9]

Aleksei

I enclose a drawing sent to me for approval by a volost elder. I approve it.

75

[Germany, March, 1906]

That Savva[10] is like me—that's not important. But that our relationship "for reasons entirely incomprehensible to you has changed"—that's important. And sad.

We must not part, since we both can be very useful to each other—quite apart from the pleasure involved. Why your attitude toward me has changed, I don't know, but I can say this for myself: The totality of my attitudes toward you is something very firm and definite, and this totality does not change either quantitatively or qualitatively, it only shifts around inside me—understand?

My life is more scattered than yours, and I am continually and indefatigably busy absorbing "impressions of life" of the most sharply varied sorts, and sometimes the abundance of these impressions, by their very massiveness, push aside what has been previously formed in the depths of my soul, but—they don't change what has been created in any essential way. This is very simple. That's all I can tell you about "relationships."

Soon I'll leave here and I too will go to Switzerland—will I meet you somewhere? I would like very much to read your play! When you get this tell Ladyzhnikov[11] where you'll be.

I'm working like a horse, as usual. I am appearing here at public readings and private banquets, but it's not worth it, and about two weeks from now I'm going straight to America.[12] Want to come? It's all the same, you can't go back to Russia now, whichever way you look at it. There's nowhere to live there. In the spring a desperate confusion will begin, there's no doubt about it.

Of course it's even worse in America than in Prussia. But maybe it's better? We'll see.

You're not judging me very profoundly. I'm a Social Democrat[13] because I am a revolutionary, and the Social Democratic doctrine is the most revolutionary. You say: "the barracks!" My friend, in every philosophy the critical part is important, while the positive part is not even always interesting, let alone important.

Anarchy is something very primitive indeed. Denial in order to affirm the absolute autonomy of my ego is splendid but just for the sake of denial is not clever. In the final analysis, anarchy is a dead end, but the human "ego" is the active beginning; even when it denies itself, this is so, and cannot be otherwise, as the Indians have shown.

It would be interesting to read the play.

I'm sitting near Berlin, I am composing political letters in Europe, and learning to talk German. I like the language. A precise language. Today I learned that such nouns as prince, lord, fool and bull all belong to the same declension.

I lectured here in the theater. A prince came and applauded me. Bülow[14] too applauded. I accept this with satisfaction and will pay them back very cruelly. People abroad give a great deal, and I am glad that I left Russia, where prison and trial were waiting for me, which might not have turned out very pleasantly. When I come back from America. I'll make a tour around Europe— that'll be nice!

You too—live here. Even I began to feel sick in Russia,

84

although I'm a hardy nag. The most unpleasant and even repulsive objects are the people with liberal convictions. A man with liberal convictions is the center of a body, including that part of it which I, living in a cultured country, must not name aloud.

Now, good-bye. Stop thinking about "relationships." If two trees stand in the forest higher than the rest, no matter how far they stand from one another they will still bow their heads to each other in a storm and will see each other in calm weather. Day and night.

Press A.M.'s[15] hand for me, she's a very dear and fine person, my greetings to her. Maruska,[16] my tongue and secretary, will write separately.

Addio!

A.

76

[*New York, April 11 (N.S.), 1906*[17]]
Hotel Belleclaire
Broadway & 77th St.
New York
Milton Roblee

Well, Leonid, here is where you must visit, I mean it. It is such an amazing fantasy of stone, glass, and iron, a fantasy constructed by crazy giants, monsters longing after beauty, stormy souls full of wild energy. All these Berlins, Parises, and other "big" cities are trifles in comparison with New York.

Socialism should first be realized here—that's the first thing you think of when you see these amazing houses, machines, etc.

And imagine, yesterday, on the first day of my arrival, I already met a socialist—a millionaire. Here, it seems, such monsters are no rarity.

And they shoot at the workers here as in all well-run states—nice, isn't it? Now there's a strike by 500 thousand coal miners. The capitalists say: we'll lose a billion, but we won't give in.

The ocean is better than Bal'mont[18] describes it, much better. The ocean is something after which you expect the unusual, the improbable, and even America does not satisfy you after the ocean. Although New York is a marvel: We live on the ninth floor of a fourteen-story building. The view from the windows is striking: Broadway stretches for about five versts. Central Park, a sea of houses, the harbor, and the Hudson River—all this is at our feet. And from the depths of dark city blocks, buildings of 28, of 33 stories, rise skyward. It is all stupendous.

I press your hand, greetings to A.M. Write.

A.

77

[United States, between April and October, 1906]

Now you said at the fjord that there were no storms; what more do you want? You lucky Russians are making a revolution at home, in your native language, and I have to do it through interpreters. Inconvenient, but just the same, it works.

My friend, America[19] is an amazingly clumsy country, and in this way it is terrifically interesting. I am glad that I came here, since even in dust bins you can find pearls—for example, the silver spoons thrown out by the cook along with the dishwater.

America is the dust bin of Europe. Now people who have left their souls somewhere at home are coming here. There is none of the kind of emigrant who would catch tigers by the tail and bite off the trunks of elephants at a gallop. And there are no elephants; there never were. Tigers are a matter for Skitalets.[20]

My dear friend, I could write ten volumes about America of 500 pages each, and not one good word! Think how unjust that is, and how good!

The Russian revolution, if you look at it even from a distance, is a splendid revolution. It has been going on for a long time. You and I shall die some time, and all the priests and all those who read liturgies over us will die, but it will go on living. Fact. You'll see.

Now we Russians will drag the world forward, while the old madame France will say:

"Ah, when I was young, I too once knocked the king's head off. . . ."

And after thinking a bit she will add, the hussy:

"But I don't remember why I did it. . . ."

And the German whom she married will say to her philosophically:

"You were young and therefore you did stupid things. I was never young and therefore love my Kaiser, although one of his arms is withered and his ear is running."

I have seen everything here: M. Twain,[21] Harvard University, missionaries, Goethals, Mark Hanna, socialists, and field mice. But I haven't seen Niagara. I won't see it. I don't want Niagara!

The best things here are two dogs, Nestor and Deory. Next the butterflies. Wonderful butterflies! The spiders are good. And the Indians.

If you haven't seen an Indian, you can't understand civilization and you can't feel a strong enough scorn for it. The Negro is not very receptive to civilization either, but the Negro loves sweets. He can serve as a doorman. The Indian can do nothing. He simply comes into the city silently, looks at civilization for a while, smokes, spits, and silently disappears. So he lives, and when the hour of his death comes he will also spit, that Indian!

Life is beautiful, my friend, that is the message of the Indian. Did you see Galien?[22] You should look at it. There is an Indian in it.

Another good thing about America are the professors, especially the psychologists. Of all the fools who are stupid precisely because they think they are clever, these are the most utter fools. One might come to America just to chat with professors of psychology. When you are sad sometime you should get into a steamer, and after lolling around for six days on the ocean you'll get out in America. A professor comes up to you, and, not offering to carry your suitcase (which he would probably be able to do artistically), he will ask you, looking at you with his left eye directed at his own right nostril:

"Do you suppose, sir, that the soul is immortal?"

And if you don't die of laughter, he will ask again:

"Is it rational, sir?"

Sometimes the skin on my back almost splits from laughter.

Prostitution and religion are interesting here. Religion is an object of comfort. One of the faithful goes up to the priest and says:

"I have heard you for three years, sir, and you have satisfied me completely. I liked it when you spoke to me in church about heaven, the angels, the future heaven, about the humble and the meek. But, sir, recently your sermons have indicated some dissatisfaction with life. That isn't good for me. In church I want to have a rest. . . . I am a businessman, a man of affairs, I need rest. And therefore it would be a very good thing, sir, if you stopped talking about the hard things of life or left the church."

The priest does either one thing or the other and everything follows its course.

But I can't write any more, although I'm enjoying this writing. Still one has to get some sleep sometime.

Until we meet, if the guns haven't got you! Greetings to dear A.M.[23] You didn't write a single word about her. All are well.

Addio!

A.

78

[Capri, Autumn, 1906]

Lazarus![24]

And again I say: this, in my view, is the best of all that has been written about death in all the world's literature. It even seems to me that you seemed to draw near and draw other people near to the insoluble riddle without solving it, but are strangely closely acquainted with it. You feel it, tranquil, dark, great in its calmness—it is amazing and good. The style is splendidly sustained. In general, as literature, as a work of art, this work gives me immense enjoyment and excites a glorious joy for you; you're a fine fellow! Philosophically, I can't accept it. I am infected by life and by its drives for six hundred years, and the longer I live the more optimistically I look on life, although my stomach and teeth hurt unbearably. But the philosophy of your story sinks into the beauty of its form as an octopus sinks into the bewitching depths of the Gulf of Naples. This gulf, and especially Capri, is beautiful and deeper than love and woman. In love you know everything at once, while here it's hardly possible to know everything. The blue grotto is truly a fairy tale, but fools and vulgar people have retold it, and therefore it's not very fascinating. But here there is a green grotto, and this is the chiseled music of Grieg, as was said by Ivan Pavlov,[25] a perceptive soul, who loves you very much, for which I love him still more.

Friend! Here there's a fisherman Spadaro, a beautiful old man whom all the artists draw. I rode out with him to catch fish, and it was much, immeasurably more marvelous and beautiful than Lazarus' visions from beyond the grave. Don't be offended. You'll come and see. I like everything here, and even the people —they're such fine fellows! They say they're swindlers. The swindling I've seen is naïve and funny but not disturbing. I think that I'll spend the winter here; I have such a mass of work that it would be useful for me to stay here. Naples is a treasury of great beauties. The Farnese Collection alone is worth a bow. In general it's good!

Coming here? What, to the Germans? That's dull, the Germans. And to Norway for the summer?

I have nothing against death, but I feel a disgust with corpses, especially with those which have not been buried for some reason, and they walk the streets, marry, write books, draw pictures, and in general remain among the living, supported by some inert strength on their two legs. Death, if it is whole, final, and complete, may be even beautiful, but dying is always repulsive, don't you think? Of course this is a truism. And I want you to hate the dying and beat them up with all the calm, immense force of your talent.

I am as far from you as a Negro from an English lord, you're right! But I love you as the Red Indian loves the night of his plains, the bewitching mist of its expanses—I'm writing stupidly, but in Italy that's forgivable, here you want to be a child, turn somersaults and cartwheels, and, lying naked for whole hours on the rocks, look at the sea, this sea which smiles even in a storm!

Just think: my stomach hurts and my tooth aches, the Frenchmen belch, the anarchists are boring, and in my hand a gay devil dances the tarantella and I'm drunk without wine. The wine here is beautiful, first of all. Then it is good and very light. You can drink a lot of it, but it is better to drink little—too bad, it glows so prettily in the glass!

I am writing a long story,[26] you won't like it, but it attracts me. Soon I'll finish it and then I'll write one happy story. Yesterday I read Gorky's play *Enemies*.[27] When I had read it, I noted to him that he had not succeeded in working on this thing, it is lightheaded and hastily done. The last-named quality is the property of Leonid Andreev, I stated, and you should not steal it from him. After talking in friendly and simple fashion, I advised him to write another play. He'll write, if he doesn't die from stomach sickness. Well, enough nonsense, I think.

How are Lady Shura and the new one?[28] Write.

Greetings. I wanted to send a letter with P–v Pov.[29] but he was bewitched here. I'm expecting Piatnitskii.[30] Greetings again.

A.

I'm sorry that you want to reconstruct "The Tsar"[31] into a play—your style for such themes is the short story and no one will write such a thing better than you, even, I think, Flaubert himself, my idol.

Leave it, won't you?

79

[*Capri, October-November*, 1906[32]]

Were I a critic I would write an article about you beginning like this:

"There's no question in my mind that L. Andreev is at present the most interesting writer in Europe and America, and I think that he is at the same time the most talented writer of the two hemispheres."

With no particular effort I would prove this by comparison and a demonstration of the breadth of your mental grasp of things and ideas. Then I would say:

"Every new work of his is a more or less significant step

forward in form and content, along a new and free road, but he hurries and his steps are uneven. He hurries too much, damn him!"

And then I would begin to show you how harmful this is for you—to hurry. And I would point out that in my opinion that is more harmful than anything else. But I'm not yet a critic.

Life of Man[33] is a superb thing as an attempt to create a new form of drama. I think that of all the efforts of this kind yours is really the most successful. It seems to me that you have taken the forms of the old mystery but have discarded the mystery heroes, with extremely interesting and original results. In places, as for example in describing the friends and enemies of the man, you introduce the simplicity and evil naïveté of a cheap religious picture; that is also your own, and it too is good. The language in this play is the best that you have ever achieved.

But—you hurried. In the life of your man, there is almost no human life, and what there is is too artificial, not real. The man therefore has turned out to be very insignificant, less and weaker than he actually was, less interesting. The man who speaks so splendidly with Him cannot live such an empty life as he lives in your play; his existence is more tragic, the dramas in his life are more frequent. In the life of your man I see one drama only: the death of his son. This is a trifle. When he gets rich, he is completely incomprehensible; is he satisfied with riches? How much? Is he dissatisfied? How much? And riches are also dramatic for a strong spirit. His (your hero's) relations toward his wife are bucolic, not natural. People don't live with their wives all their lives as if they were just friends, and that's the way you have shown him; why?

Now I have met an odd fellow, the famous artist Diffenbakh.[34] In one of his pictures he painted himself in this way: he is dragging a heavy cross up a mountain. On the end of the cross his wife is sitting, and a church lashes him with a whip while it upholds his wife. This is of course too coarse as a symbol, but it is reality. You say: I don't want reality! Understand (I am speaking about content, not form), it cannot but be real; I hope this needs no proof.

In general, you have stripped your man down too much, removing him from reality and in this way depriving him of tragedy, flesh, and blood. All this has been written with too much emphasis on the form, and I can't avoid the natural desire to emphasize the insignificance, the incompleteness, the poverty of the life of your man. I also note that the presence of old women in the first act recalls *L'Intruse* by Maeterlinck. The old women are hard to understand; what are they? You told I.P.[35] that they are lesser fates (*podsud'binki*), but lesser fates, as Afanas'ev[36] points out, symbolize not only the forces of nature hostile to man but primarily represent those things in life which people think are chance happenings but which result from a chain of causes arising from the relations between people and thus become logically necessary. The last act is beautiful, a picture, but the old women hinder us from understanding it and ruin the tragedy of the end of life. I also cannot understand why you chose a tavern as the place for your man's final downfall. Why not a church? Not the square where he begins his fight with Him before the people's eyes. My certainty of the force of your talent tells me that you might have written this very significant work still better than you wrote it. There. But you hurry. Where to? You haven't anywhere to rush to, believe me. No one values you as I do, and I know that you are not writing just for the present, and I emphasize this. You will not only be read in the future but will be studied. For this reason I keep urging you, without success, to treat yourself with great respect, you German devil!

I am glad that here the Mediterranean Sea is like Niagara as it too is incomparably greater and more magnificent than all that has been said and written about it. The people are crooks but nice, dirty but beautiful, avaricious but childlike. They use money primarily for gambling. Capri is a tiny crumb, but delicious. Only the gnats bite at night. You see so much here at once all the time, in one day, which is beautiful that you get drunk, stagger around, and can do nothing. You keep looking and smiling. It's not expensive. This might be where Lady Shura[37] could rest up and get well! Think this over.

Well, good-bye for the present! Warm embraces. I congratulate you, kiss Shura on both paws, and also embrace your mamma. My respects also to all your people. All the best, friend! Write!

When you plan to come telegraph me in Capri.

Everyone here sends greetings along with mine.

A.

80

[*Capri, late* 1906–*early* 1907]

K.P.,[38] who is soon going to Finland, will write you, or talk with you personally, about the limitations of your power, and I will speak of literature.

My attitude toward Blok[39] is negative, as you know. This lad, who is making a Russian adaptation of the bad half of Paul Verlaine, recently has definitely disturbed me with his cold mannerisms; his small talent is positively exhausted under the load of philosophical travail. This is undermining the strength of this self-confident boy, who is overeager for glory and has a soul without trousers and without a heart. No. Leave him in peace for about three years; maybe he will grow up in that time and learn how to speak sincerely about simple things, which now seem to him amazingly profound and which have already been expressed in France more strongly and beautifully than he could do it.

The old flirt Sologub[40] has been in love with death as lackeys are in love with their mistresses and he flirts with her always in the alarmed expectation of getting a rap on the skull from her. Sologub, who is inclined to sadism, is not necessary in the *Znanie* volume. Be kind and don't disturb his last days, and you can be sure that he will not write another *Little Devil* (the only thing he has written as creative literature, with love and, beautiful in its own way). I don't see what more Auslander[41] has to say, but I have nothing against him, as I have nothing against Somov,[42] for example.

I would ask you to think about the words "liberation of man," words which you used in a letter to me. They have an extremely

93

profound significance; the people you have named for this "liberation" are not strong enough to serve. They are all old slaves, people who *cannot* avoid confusing freedom with pederasty. For example, for them "liberation of man" in some strange way is confused with moving him from one sink into another, and in time they descend to liberating one organ and no more.

The *Znanie* volumes are volumes of democratic literature and for democracy; only in democracy and by its force will man be liberated. A true individualism, worthy of man, is alone capable of liberating the personality from its dependence on and captivity by society and the State and will be attained only through socialism, *i.e.,* through democracy. We should serve it and arm it with our boldness to think about everything without fear, speak without terror.

The Sologub and Blok you mentioned fear their own imagination, and fall on their knees before their fear—how can they liberate man!

Zaitsev,[43] Bashkin,[44] Muizhel',[45] Tsenskii,[46] Lansberg,[47] L. Semënov,[48] and some more of the newcomers—those are the people, to my mind, whom you might use to make good volumes.

Some of them love literature sincerely and warmly and do not clothe themselves in it to call the reader's attention to the insignificance and poverty of their "Ego"—which the others, in their thoughts, always pronounce with a capital letter, wishing in this way to exaggerate its significance, since how else could they exaggerate it?

The poor in spirit are a very repulsive people!

Here it is amazing. I swim, catch fish, write.

Too bad you have undertaken this building;[49] in a year it will be unbearably revolting for you, and in two you'll set it on fire. Don't forget to buy insurance, as experienced people do.

I read a lot of "new" literature: Kuzmin's *Northern Almanacs, White Nights, The Scales,*[50] and so on. I'm sure that twenty-five years ago I would have liked it.

I press your hand. Write.   *A.*

81

[*St. Petersburg,*] *February* 11 [, 1908[51]]

My dear Alekseiushka!

I am now sitting quietly in St. Petersburg resting in all possible directions and feel as if I had sat for a year in some place like Port Arthur, or, like Dante, had traveled a year in hell. And when I look back on the year 1907, I think: Man is indeed determined to live! Of course, now I have occupational asthma, and my head is like the Jewish quarter after a pogrom, and my legs are like twisted bolts—but is that real payment for all that I have done and all that has happened to me? There was a whole month when my reason was completely confused. Then dejection, amazing dejection, when I sometimes felt that I had reached the ultimate *bounds of grief*, those mysterious limits which separate grief from something new and unattainable, neither life nor death. Then I drank, for three or four days, at first from wineglasses and then cognac from tumblers. Then women, one soap bubble after another, whom I chased, lifting up my weeping drunken face; they left the taste of cheap soap on my tongue and on my heart.

Work? No, I don't consider that I worked this year. "Darkness"[52] is a brutally unsuccessful and confused story. "The Curse of the Beast"[53] is a sort of spiritual putty which I used to keep the draft from blowing so strongly through the crack. Finally *King Hunger*[54] itself is only a third as well written as it should have been and sometimes stinks like a corpse buried in the grave. Yes, there is something dead and cold about it. In places it is good, but the background is gray, bad. That is all that has been accomplished, essentially nothing or almost nothing, since *King Hunger* is still not all bad.

Now I am not drinking and apparently beginning to live again. Has anything changed? No. I am just as lonely, I still have no woman whom I could love, the apartment is just as empty and echoing as it was, like a hospital. And I have no friend except you, so far off and so unreliable. Some sort of crisis apparently took place, and my life is beginning to climb upward, and that quality which made Shura[55] call me "Vanka-Stand-Up" is reappearing. Well! if I have paid for Shura's death with only what has already happened to me, it would be terribly cheap.

Although it seems to me my really great sufferings are beginning only now, on the way back. There is no contradiction here. Tragedy is an affirmation of life, and only drama excludes life. And what has saddened me in the past year, in terms of individual motives, was just drama, no more, just a rather horrible and dirty petty drama. Only reporters and bad writers call suicide a tragedy, and I think that among the millions of suicides none could be found who would be truly tragic. The people of tragedy are living and only the people of drama kill themselves.

The tragedy was my life on Capri,[56] at the beginning, when I wandered alone over the island and listened to the storms. And it will become a tragedy in the spring, when once for all I leave this detestable city with its wretched bustle and once for all come face to face with nature, with the sea, the sky, the snow, face to face with pure human thought. How I love my future country house[57]! Doesn't this love disturb you? It is not the love an owner has for his property, you understand, but something else. One has to live either the way you live or the way I want to live: either stand in the very whirlpool of life and create it, or retreat a distance from it and try to think about it. My spirit inclines toward the second alternative. It seems to me that I have seen and felt and even known enough, since, drunk or sober, gay or sad, I have never stopped looking, and whole trunks full of observations lie within me and I have already absorbed a great deal and give away nothing. To give obliges one to comprehend, and how can I do that when thousands of windmills whir their arms before my nose, when I lose perspective from my closeness to things, and Artsybashev's[58] impotent organ covers the moon and the stars, when the voice of the policeman rings in my ears louder than the voice of God himself, and so on and so forth. I want to understand, to understand, but I have seen enough.

For half a year now some sort of crisis has been growing more acute; it is becoming so obvious that I can write nothing serious. I have felt the old, and I do not know the way to the new. And what the new consists of I also don't know. Undoubtedly it is only that I have somehow suddenly turned from the rejection of life to the affirmation of it, and while I formerly thought that only death exists, now I am beginning to guess that there is only life. And just to guess. It is striking, for example, to me that along with the sufferings which I have already described sufficiently I have been feeling almost constantly an immense, monstrous joy in life. While I used to look gloomily at the successes of the revolution and croaked, so it was, so it will be, now, living in the shadow of the gallows, I now feel joy and invincible confidence in the triumph of life. It seems to be turning out as it did with the fool who laughed at the funeral and wept at the wedding, but it is not that, not that. And what it is I don't know, I don't know, and I won't know until I have left the vanities of life, and in the wild variety of impressions I may perceive some majestic unity still unknown to me.

That is why I so love my future house with all its facilities for solitude and work. . . . But now something amazingly stupid is turning up; it may be happening because I am basically too healthy. Good God! Like the most ordinary, vulgar, typical healthy fellow, I have to be well fed and warm and have a wife and children, for my *thoughts* to be free and not occupied with flattery. I remember that when I was a young student I could think only of food. And now it has turned out like this: deprived of a woman for whole months (just imagine, for whole months!) I could think only of women and in a special way, no worse than Artsybashev. Of course, I could make arrangements, as others do: hire a maid (the doctors have even advised this), go to the whorehouse on Saturdays, or simply take advantage of the numerous offers that reach me in the local mail. But I cannot; this repels me. I need a wife, not only a body but a soul, that special type of woman's soul which cannot be replaced by a thousand male souls, as a thousand cigarette holders, let's say, do not replace a single cigarette. The comparison is not completely successful, but you know what I mean. For the same reasons, masturbation is not acceptable. Of course, there is another way: to rise above it, conquer the flesh and chop up the spirit. But whether or not I could do it, I would not want to do it. By mortification and chopping I would pull the chair out from under my philosophic outlook, and I would endanger something no less valuable than my process of thought.

I am going to interrupt this letter abruptly at this point, since, if I don't finish today (and it is now three a.m. and I am tired) the accumulation of my vanity will not let me stop soon. Better to continue later. I shall only say that I love you well and truly. And there is lots more that I must write.

I press your hand.

Your Leonid

82

[*Capri, early* 1908 (?)][59]

You should come here, Leonid, and live here, until your house is built; there's nothing for you to do in this market of the poor, who trade in stolen rags and the dirty cast-offs of their rotten souls.

Just look what all these savages are doing with you (now your comrades in common labor): their founder, Merezhkovskii,[60] walks with dirty feet over your face; Hippius[61] has slandered you in *Mercure de France;* and in Briusov's journal[62] you are called a boor and a fool—that's not criticism, but organized slander, vile slander, something unprecedented in our literature.

They are pulling Kuprin[63] into your place, only because he is less talented than you and not so terrifying to the pygmies, as he won't crush them. And he, poor fellow, has already become confused, and after "The Emerald" he has saddled Solomon and pranced about on him like a high-school boy, to his own disgrace. And you are all confused before the onslaught of the barbarian hordes and their hungry ambition and the slyness of the degenerates.

Throw up all this Sologubism[64] for a while; understand that it is not worthy of you, with your talent, to submit involuntarily to their infectious influence and to write such things as "Darkness."[65] I almost roared when I read this tar smooch and then was angry with you for sixteen years. Ah, my boy.

98

Keep in mind from now on: they will go on slandering you more vilely until they meet with adequate resistance, which probably we must provide, I mean from our side. We are organizing a number of literary-critical volumes, and although Gornfel'd[66] has said that "nothing good should be expected from the SDs," Gornfel'd is not of the wisest prophets. All this brightly dressed *bourgeoisie* who call themselves the "bearers of true culture" struggle for the first row in the theater of life, but they won't get there. They are weak and late, and even if you keep on helping them as diligently as you have up to now, their song is finished, and they have been exposed quite sufficiently to display to all their incurably infected soul.

Come here; I mean it. It's good here. But in Petersburg you are tormented and wasted.

You're a strange fellow! Well, can you, for example, stay in the place where Sologub has vomited his own "magic"?[67] Is it possible that you don't see how stupid and dirty that is? Is it?

I'm sorry about Kuprin. What is he doing? This "Sulamith" of his is incredibly bad. But—you'll see—he'll be praised even for that. He must be. We have almost no literature, only lust.

Come here, you!

And don't think I want to fight with you about *Znanie*; I just want you to rest from this trashy squabbling.

Aleksei

83

[*St. Petersburg, March* 23, 1908][68]

My dear Alekseiushka!

I have not changed, so don't change your attitude toward me. In "Darkness"[69] (apart from its weakness in form) and in *King Hunger*[70] I am the same as I was in *Savva*[71] and "Judas."[72] And I am the same when I work for *Shipovnik*[73] as I was when I worked for *Znanie*.[74] My comrades—no, they are not my comrades. And as for editing the *Almanac*, I am starting right off by refusing to publish the continuation of *Fairy Magic*.[75] And I don't care for any of them, except perhaps for Blok.[76] Probably I will leave

Briusov[77] out of the future volumes; let him go his own way. And if we had, really had, talented writers of the former *Znanie* type, not used up or worn out or aged (like that nice Serafimovich)[78] I would form a group of them only.

I shall try. If it does not turn out, I will throw it aside, but I won't permit any corruption.

I am not coming to Capri now. It is far to go, and the approaching Petersburg spring, which I love, is calling me. But in the fall I shall come, if I survive. Now I am working hard. I am writing a long story, three or four signatures long, "The Seven Who Were Hanged,"[79] about the death penalty. I feel that there is no real protest, and I want to shout, "Don't hang them, you rabble!" The individual characters in the story aren't bad, but I don't know how it will turn out as a whole. It is hard to write.

Yes, the slander against me would have been unprecedented, if it were not for your starting it all.[80]

From top to bottom, on all floors of the Russian literary mansion (which sometimes very much resembles a house of pleasure), I am slandered. There is even some organization in this: the magazine *The Scales*[81] and the Merezhkovskiis[82] are carrying out a deliberate policy, and Kuprin[83] is being systematically praised. But more of it is on the spur of the moment, sincere and unperceptive.

Yes, slander. The Cadets, the mystics, the Decadents, the Octobrists, the Black Hundreds—from all sides. But I never expected that the Social Democrats would top off the slander and that to the names of Merezhkovskii, Hippius,[84] and Briusov would be added that of Lunacharskii[85] in *The Decay of Literature*, a publication endorsed with your name and your authority.

"Cowardly slave," "petty bourgeois," "slanderous depiction of the working class," "*King Hunger* is the revolution as it is reflected in the mind of a petty bourgeois, an artist maybe but still a hopeless petty bourgeois."

I am not sorry for myself. I am sorry for the work which is done by such methods as Lunacharskii's, in servile fashion. They talk of themselves as if they were participants in a new, perfect life, a new psychology, but they write and think like the *New Times* people.[86]

Where Lunacharskii is only a fool, he has little effect on me, and even in their own lives fools remain fools. When he confuses "rebellion" with revolution (just for these gentlemen I added the sentence in *King Hunger;* "Do not slander the revolution, this is rebellion," but it was of no use), and it is on this and only this misunderstanding that he bases his accusation that I am petty bourgeois, I can take it calmly. The time is not far off when I shall write *Revolution* (it will be the third in a cycle of plays, and this has already been mentioned in print), and then even Lunacharskii will understand that by immortality I mean more than he does and that I fear death less than he. And I value the proletariat even more highly than he does.

But there is one place in his article where he writes: "Andreev's revolutionaries burn the National Gallery. This has never been and never shall be. The revolutionary proletariat always protects museums. These details fill out the picture of Andreev's powerlessness in the face of revolution."

Andreev said:

Engineer: These people have burned down something else, apparently. The National Gallery. What idiots! But *it is very possible that our own troops set fire to the Gallery.*

Lunacharskii:

"Andreev's mobs work alongside the workers and combine revolution (revolution again! what a fool!) with robbery. This is an *unscrupulous lie.* The mob either became civil guards and shot down the workers, or they thundered under the banner of monarchy and religion, like our Black Hundreds. Whenever the revolution has triumphed (Lord, what a fool!) the mobs have trembled."

Andreev:

Engineer: And among these beggars we found some rather clever and quick rascals who could be bought cheap, and we gave them instructions of a rather intimate nature. And at present these idiots have already begun to exterminate one another in the most splendid fashion.

I don't know your views, but I find this portrayal no less distorted than Burenin's[87] and Merezhkovskii's.

You wrote quite recently: "Keep in mind from now on: they will go on slandering you more vilely until they meet with adequate resistance, which probably we must provide, I mean from our side."[88]

So, Alekseiushko. Sad, this.

Your Leonid

I'll go on about *The Decay of Literature*.

The most important task of the modern farce is to analyze where the enemies are and where the friends. Thoughts lie, words lie, everything is disguised. Lunacharskii uses the word "petty bourgeois" and Kamenskii[89] uses the same word. If you don't walk naked, with your organ exposed, you must be a petty bourgeois. "Petty bourgeois," if you don't use the back door for the "sacred purpose of Eros," "boor" (*i.e.,* also petty bourgeois), if you reject God, the devil, or Merezhkovskii and his wife.

And it is very sad that the compilers of *The Decay of Literature* have not made as clear as they should where the enemies are and where the friends. With idiotic diligence, like Lunacharskii, they beat up their own side, again vulgarizing and depriving of meaning the concept of the petty bourgeois, by the way. And they accuse Briusov of being bourgeois in a friendly way, almost with a caress. And if it is properly analyzed, is there a more characteristic representative of "their literature" than this same Briusov? A contributor to *Russian News* in Kozetskii's time,[90] patriot and almost a chauvinist, with all the demonism of arms folded across his chest, with his decorative poems and his laments for culture, with his she-goat,[91] with Ellis,[92] Kuzmin,[93] and Feofilaktov,[94] he is the true hero of the petty bourgeoisie. And you know this well yourself. He is very talented, but only when he is an instrument for the writing of verse, an artificial mechanism which is taken apart at night and stored in kerosene and in the morning smeared with grease. When he should be a man he is simply an animal.

And these plunderers, Merezhkovskii, Hippius, and other mystics and *Kulturtraegers*? While the revolution was moving forward they dragged it back, by the tail, and now they have appeared in the field of battle and plundered the killed. It was not they who enriched and stained with blood the earth which they now try to sow with the seed of their mysticism and their religious lechery. Why have they not been resisted?

"Fear of death," says Lunacharskii. All right, can he show a single case, a single line in my writings when I have bowed to even one of the bourgeois idols because of this fear? And when for any reason at all, even for an instant, have I supported the bourgeois order? Oh, Lord! Here the Cadets, through Galich's[95] lips, call me a petty bourgeois (because I load the guilt on to one class) and the Peaceful Reformers[96] are abusing me (see the enclosed clipping).

And still on the whole your volume is good and timely.

There's no time, brother, to write. I have married and am going to the Crimea. Details by letter.

I am beginning to like being slandered.

Your Leonid Andreev

84

[Capri, late 1909–early 1910][97]

My dear Leonid!

You were wrong to think that you'd offend me by refusing to edit the volumes[98]; I'm only too pleased by your decision. If you remember, I didn't defend very warmly your idea that you should take the position of editor and pointed out that you would have to expect a pile of assorted acquaintances and a stupifying job of reading manuscripts, at least forty pounds of them a week.

Seriously, you must not think of undertaking editing in the form and sense that you have imagined. With the morbid egotism which Russian writers are sweating so profusely now, could you say successfully to any of them, without being insulted, "You have written this coldly, without love for the work"? Now everyone is writing superbly, each one believes that he is at least a sage and in any case the creator of a "new style," and they all act in the field of letters like calves in the kitchen garden: frisky. I don't think that squabbles with such a wild company could have good results.

Let's leave the editing to K.P.[99] He has the love, the taste, and the willingness for this work. And we ourselves will make literature, to the extent it is within our power.

I read all the Russian journals, and sometimes I'm sad till I almost cry, and sometimes I laugh till I'm almost mad. How scanty and insincere it all is! Look at the friendly choir of writers who are singing the dirge of the Russian revolution, for which they have already dug a grave in the arid deserts of their imagination. Now they are endeavoring to bury this young creature alive. Look at what Z. Hippius[1] writes in *The Scales*, No. 7, about you and culture, and then analyze carefully the editorial note to Zinochka's clumsy and ornate prattle—how ridiculous and insolent it all is!

Kuzmin,[2] an apparently barely literate man, who doesn't know how to write coherently and isn't acquainted with the Russian language, is the creator of a new culture, apparently! That isn't ironic.

To hell with them. They provoke me, those hundred-horse-power petty bourgeois. By the way, note their peculiarity: they talk but don't prove anything; they can't prove anything. Their method of discussion is the hysterical shrieking of an old maid.

You know that I do value this group's love for the language, I respect its vital interest in literature, I admit its substantial service to culture. It has enriched the language with a mass of new word combinations, it has created marvelous poetry, and for all this I must express thanks, from the bottom of my heart, and history too will thank them in time.

But they imagine themselves to be district supervisors in the literature department, and, like all Russian policemen, they have lost respect for individuality and individual freedom. They are offensively egotistical, that's what repels me; they are cold, they are too much the spectators of life and are always striving for the honor of being acknowledged by a "big audience," *i.e.,* by petty people.

You say Blok[3] is talented. He's written a book that's not bad, *Poems about the Beautiful Lady*. That's all so far. *The Showman* and *The Stranger* are jokes; even a drunkard won't praise him for them. Also it's naïve. And anyway, it isn't worth it.

I don't know what you understand democracy to be, but judging by what you write, I fear that you have narrowed this concept almost down to "Narodnikism",[4] may it perish in peace!

For me, democracy is faith in the potential, creative strength of the mass of the people, which like the universe is the source of all possibilities and can create Tolstoys and Leonardo da Vincis, Aeschyluses and Shakespeares. Life then is a creative process and full of amazingly unexpected things, like the fourth comet, Grieg, Andreev, etc. My definition is coarse and superficial, but I have no time to develop it because of—the comet! How splendid it is! Here I can see with my naked eye its seven-foot tail—imagine how terrifically beautiful it is? I look at it every night and it clears my head and my spirits marvelously.

The weather here is superb and the sea is beyond all words! Every day I knock about for four hours or so in a boat with the fishermen. I've caught several hundred fish, and wrote "The Spy."[5] It came out long and dull, but that didn't bother me; I had to write this thing, it was on my mind. Now I'll write a story "The Artist," or something on that theme. A free man passes through a revolution and in passing helps it to be completed. That's all.

But the best thing of all is the comet, Leonid. Eventually we men will look beyond the limits of our atmosphere (why not admit this, if we admit that Kuzmin is serving culture?) and look at comets near to.

We'll also walk on the bottom of the sea, among the seaweed, cliffs, and wrecked ships, like short walks on holidays. Without guides or Cook, of course. Soon I'll go to Florence, only I have no money. I live like a rich man, in debt.

And about anger and various insults—drop it once for all. It's legal to get mad, but not over trifles. I love you and can admire you, and that gives me an advantage which is as pleasant and stirring as a fine night with restless thousands of bright stars.

Don't give me compliments, you've made so many of them you could use them to gild a small altar screen in a rural church. Why this luxury?

I'm sorry abuot *Navukhodonossor* [*sic*].[6] I think you'll spoil him in the play. And what you don't spoil the directors with their actors will finish off. Some blubbermouth with crooked knees who believes in God and is full of sacred trembling before Mr. Policeman will play the tsar, and when he says: "I am the Tsar!" you, the author, will hear in his words something quite different, I assure you!

Someone with malicious intent told me how *Life*[7] was performed in Terioki, and I laughed. Those are devils! They still sneeze into their napkins, although *Speech*[8] asserts that we are at the dawn of culture. Well, good-bye, however. I press your hand, embrace you with all my heart, want you to work fast, and—work!

A.

85

[*Finland, August 12, 1911*][9]

Dear Aleksei!

Of course I'm nervous about sending you this letter and using this name, and I'll probably write something confused, at least the first time. Several years of heavy silence lie between us and there is much that must be said before our former understanding, our former knowledge of one another, can be restored. And with this I'll begin: I'll tell you truly what I'm like now, both in general and in my attitude toward you.

It seems to me that I have remained just the same, both in general and especially in my attitude toward you. What I once thought, I still think now, what I once loved I still love now; and perhaps everything has just become harder, steadier, coarser, and more definite with the years. Consciousness has crept through my whole soul, and has eaten away at the dark places; little naïveté is left, and the many tracks have merged into a single straight, iron, and inevitable track, as they do when the train pulls away from a station. Of course, griefs have been added with the years; I've become sadder, darker, as if I had donned mourning, but this is truer of my personal life, my character, than of my views. I think though that even in my personal life, under somewhat more favorable conditions, I could get back my former gaiety, my insatiable and gay longing to live. Recent years have tormented me, and very frequent headaches make me unbearably morose. And it's not the headache itself, of course, that's horrible, but that it stops me from working, tears me from my desk, forces me to be idle, and makes me feel upset and hopeless about any big project and almost any work.

As before, I have no friends, except for you. You are always my friend, and in this I am so immutable that I cannot even conceive of any other feeling for you. I love you both concretely, as one can only love a good brother (even more), and abstractly, as a man, that is, I respect you. I love you very much. And through all these years of silence you have occupied in my life a position no less living than a man living by my side, very closely and alive. Strangely enough, it seems that there hasn't been a day when I wasn't thinking of you in one way or another; and in many conversations I have had with people whom I knew would be dull and boring, I was talking passionately with you; I had only you in mind, and wanted only your approval and agreement. What did it matter that you weren't here; my sense of you and my will toward you are no less a reality than your presence or absence. But that's just a consolation, and even if it's true it doesn't always help; once you've talked you also want to listen.

And believe me, Aleksei, I can't imagine what point of view would justify your being hostile, or even opposed to me. I have enough external errors in my life, and I know most of them, but my errors aren't me. On the contrary, by the nature of all my feelings and thoughts and all my life I certainly consider myself your unalterable and true ally. I repeat, I have not changed. As you once loved me, so I remain; not a single new feature that is hostile to you has come to life either in my spirit or on my face.

It is madness to think that such friends, such brothers as you and I have been, have suddenly parted, have been suddenly orphaned, and in the cruel desert of life have almost lost all trace of one another. Except for the gossipy newspapers and for slander, and of course for such friends as A. N. Tikhonov[10] (he tells me a lot about your life, and very well), we would completely lose sight of each other. But the newspapers and the slander only part us, and our own work itself doesn't exhibit the same vital link; it is as if some cloud had concealed the clear outlines of our thoughts and words and had placed on all the seal of uncertainty and questioning.

What parted us? When I try to answer this question myself, I suddenly begin to feel that special disturbance in the brain which always comes with the approach of trifles: there's no reason but there are many excuses, and each excuse is nothing in itself, but as a whole it's deep water, a mist, the wearisome irritation of some ugly dream. Perhaps, and I may be mistaken, perhaps you know the reason, but I cannot find it. Isn't the reason in fact that nightmarish matter of *Znanie*, which Piatnitskii[11] started, from beginning to end? Isn't the reason my last letter, in which, without reproaching you in any way, I asked you to tell me: do you agree with Lunacharskii,[12] your fellow contributor to the volume, when he sharply condemned me, or was that all chance? True, you didn't answer my letter and the years of silence set in . . . but still for me there are absolutely no reasons.

I've been planning to write you many times. Last year when I was in Italy, I wanted terribly to see you, but I was afraid. I wasn't even afraid of anything serious, since I don't see it that way, but of that heavy embarrassment which could occur after these years of silence and which would prevent a good talk. Finally I was far from sure that you would want to see me. And I've been writing this letter for almost a month; I could write for even a year and still not be certain that I am writing as I should and what I should. But surely we can't leave it like this —it strains the reason.

For now I'll send you what I've written; if I tried to say everything it would again take months. Answer me, tell me the *reason*, or, if you want, say nothing about the past. One way or another it has passed, and only the present demands an answer.

Just say that you trust me the way you used to, and nothing more is necessary. But even if you don't answer, I won't take back a word of this letter and I'll love you as I have up until now: in silence.

I might say too that I myself am not particularly anxious to talk over our personal affairs in so far as they belong in the past. And it's very possible that I wouldn't have gotten around to writing you for a very long time yet if I had not been prompted not only by my feeling for you but by other considerations, facts, and events in which we both appear as only Gorky and Andreev. It always seemed to me that our hostility and our friendship are not only our own personal affairs, and this is particularly clear now when Russian literature is dispersed, when our forces are so terribly disunited, when youth and talent wander without a guide, and when only one thing is demanded and wanted: unification. It would be an unforgivable mistake, it seems to me, in the view of the present and the future if we continue to stand aloof and don't join forces for the common goal. The genuine reaction, which lives in a weary heart, has already passed; far ahead of us still looms the crest of the wave which we must mount again and again. The appearance of Russia is sad, her works are trifling or shoddy, and where does the gay summons to the new, difficult work of revolution rise up? And actually now only the asses are sulking in Russia, and the clever people are already gay. The time of friendship, the time of engagements, the time of happy marriages—so the fortune-teller would say. Far from everyone knows this, but even those who don't recognize it are attracted to each other, seek alliances, and ask for new unifying slogans, since the brand of dissension and hostility lies on the old ones. Who will gather them together? That's the only question. If you were living in Russia now, you would again play the same wandering role you once played with the *Znanie* volumes; you would again rally the people. Probably you're not following this closely, but I see by innumerable details, even ordinary clumsy conversations, how your name is growing again, rising on the banks like a river after it has been damned. And those for whom it is customary will probably begin to hate you still more; this shows how much you are needed now for the work. I see no other man, a writer, who could lead the literary youth to revolutionary unity, except for you. And it's an irreparable misfortune that you're abroad now.

I heard from Tikhonov that you have already begun the work of unification (and I recently saw the issue of *The Contemporary*[13] which confirms it). Of course, you can do a lot that way, but still *The Contemporary* alone isn't enough: you need a still more vital, fundamental link with the new literature which cannot be given in a journal which is inspired from abroad. How to create this link: through piecemeal writers' congresses or a single big congress or the establishment in Russia of some very good, very active and authoritative man (only not me, of course, or it will appear that I'm recommending myself as a first-class editor)— I still don't know. We'll have to think and talk a lot about this. But each passing day more imperiously demands an answer.

Oh, Aleksei! I now definitely don't believe that we ever quarreled, that I'm forty years old with four days over—or even that my head is cracking, I don't believe it. I'm young at heart, as I was in those far distant times, and it seems to me that the address for this letter isn't Capri but Nizhnii, and in general I want to be in on the fight. My characteristic honorable moroseness sits ruffled on the sidelines, while I dally almost outside time and space. Don't condemn me for frivolity; God knows it's a sign of the greatest depth of thought and it is extremely serious, regardless of its gay attire. And don't condemn me for writing on the typewriter, my handwriting has become completely confused and the violence of my character makes me write only endless m,m,m, with hooks on them. For clarity I've taken to the typewriter, and now I've grown used to it, it's like a wife.

If you want to answer, my regular address is: Finland, Terioki, L. N. Andreev. It is best to write by registered mail via Stockholm.

I have a lot more that I want to write you.

I kiss you.

Your Leonid

August 12, 1911

86

[Capri, Autumn, 1911][14]

And my attitude toward you, Leonid, has not changed essentially and deeply, it is all the same as it has been, you are as dear to me, as interesting, as you were, and I have not stopped expecting great things from you; I believe in your talent, I know its value, and I love it. I am not saying all this out of any desire to cover over the crack in our relationship; what has been has been, and whether it will be rubbed away or grow in size is not our business. Neither of us will start lying to each other or become artificial, I'm sure.

And why it happened I'll say now: first, "Darkness".[15] I got mad at you because of it, since with this story you stole from the poor Russian public the alms fate had given it. The incident actually took place, but not as you have described it; it was better, more humane, and more significant. The girl turned out to be better than the man, who had stopped being a revolutionary and was afraid to reveal this to himself and to others. It was a holiday, a triumph of man over cattle, but you played with anarchy and made the cattle and the darkness triumph over the human. Then, "My Notes."[16] This was also offensive, first, because it coincides with the "philosophy" of that stupid Chulkov,[17] secondly because it preaches a passive attitude toward life, a doctrine which I didn't expect and which is not consistent with you.

The misfortune of our country undoubtedly lies in the fact that we have been poisoned by the thick, heavy blood of the East; this is what inclines us to reflect our own vileness and powerlessness passively, to gossip about eternity, space, and any other higher materials for "self-perfection" and other lengthy trifles. In addition, we as a nation have been tormented by our clumsy history, are incapable of continuous and steady effort, because we are wearied from disillusion; we have lost hope, we don't know who to believe, and waver from fanaticism to nihilism. This is in each of us and in everyone, this is the first thing we would have to fight, a mutilation which corrupts the soul, blocks the free growth and blossoming of the personality, and lowers our capacity. You must love Russia, must rouse her energy, her consciousness of her beauty, her strength, her feeling of self-respect; she must be inoculated with a feeling of the joy of existence—mustn't she? Well, "My Notes" is not in agreement with this. Nor is "Darkness" either.

Furthermore, there is no doubt that you had to smell how horrible glory smelled! well, good, smell; But after smelling it, kick it aside with your foot, chase it out of the house, and hire a good housemaid, who would simply understand that you are a man, who thinks of the things that all men all over the world think of and who understands that you need peace and quiet and that a chambermaid would be more useful and pleasant for you than glory. But you were attracted. Merezhkovskii,[18] this trained flea now elevated to a "thinker," was right when he wrote about you that you were squeezed in "the monkey's paws." Of course, some clever man whispered this to him, maliciously, but —how was I to read his article about you, written in the tone of an old hag who has been permitted to speak openly and is listened to with attention?

I can curse you too because I love literature, and as I do— don't be offended—but these Merezhkovskiis, your judges, and Chukovskiis,[19] your lackeys, and all this loud-mouthed rabble, shouting about you from all sides—this offended me, and listening to their dissonant howling I knew, with great pain I knew, that they would betray you, that they would give you a shove and rough you up.

This almost happened, and you helped them along yourself, by your own free will.

The Russian writer should be a sacred person; in Russia there is nothing to marvel at, no one to bow to, except the writer. The Russian writer, each time covetous and dirty hands want to embrace him, should exclaim: "Off! I know myself who I am in my own country!" In my own country, Leonid, say that, because we have covered its wounds and scars with our own hearts, and our hearts, stretched over it, have been trampled by the hooves of cattle, you know that already. You have cut the distance between yourself and the "mulish rabble," and have degraded the meaning of literature (not you alone, of course, Kuprin[20] too, and many many more). But many perhaps have followed your example: If Andreev himself does this, we can too.

And then you sent a telegram to Iasinskii[21]—ugh! I don't doubt that you did not read a single line of his writings, under the name of "Irinirkh Plutarkhov," *First of March*, etc., and you of course did not know who this dirty, malicious old man is in Russian literature and what he deserves. But Leonid Andreev caressing Ieronim Iasinskii—that, brother, is a dark picture!

Thus, as you see, I agree with Lunacharskii[22]; he was right in abusing you, say what you will; a fact remains a fact. You took some part too in the general dance on the graves, in the general confusion, and you got confused to the extent that you considered Iasinskii a person worthy of your attention. All this, surely, is not praiseworthy, all this is a chain of errors; you hurried, you lowered your own price, and decreased the attention you received.

But I have nothing to say about *Znanie;* I agree with the challenge to Piatnitskii.[23] Yes, he is ill, this log, he has decayed from within. I wasn't annoyed for a minute by your withdrawal from *Znanie*, but it is too bad you fell into Tseitlin's[24] hands. That man has been at my place; his strong point is money, but intelligence God did not give him.

That's how I feel about you, that's a list of the wounds I have received at your hand.

Won't you stop talking about it? Must you explain yourself? I wouldn't advise it, words don't convince me and never did, but—let's try to cook some new porridge together, altogether new.

I live more in Russia than you do, and I don't have a very great faith in any "improvement of attitude." This improvement must be created, but you can't count on it. For the present the "improvement" is expressed by a tenser mood of expectation than there was two or three years ago: won't someone attack us? This desire to get a push from without, from the sidelines, is obvious evidence that within ourselves, inside, we don't yet have energy free for the fight. And this is our immediate task and job: to gather our scattered energy, to free it from the nets and chains of various doubts, fears, skepticism, etc., all nonsense.

This work—if we could only get on with it!—would restore significance to Russian literature and would again put it in a position from which it has been removed by various "practitioners."

Already the former supporters of "pure art," like Briusov,[25] have begun to complain of the gulf between poetry and life; a natural development, it should have been expected of course. Naturally in this case I am not talking about "tendencies" and "programs," but of the spirit, of the mood: writers felt (and some were even deeply stirred by it) their solitude in their native country, in life, and the tragedy of this solitude has some-how come to be understood; we may expect that from "eternity," "limitless space," "fatal contradiction of the sexes," and all other such dark closets the public will begin to creep out into the light, to attain freedom to argue for itself and its right to live well, as a man should.

Man is still the center of my concern, and even in cursing him I still love him—a wonderful beast! If only he were not so lazy and could understand this beauty of movement better!

But we must talk over all these profundities nose to nose.

A congress?[26] Well, a congress is possible. But first it would be good for the two of us to get together or write each other about it in detail. Write me what you imagine the congress should be like, who, when, where, etc.

I think success is possible. I have always thought that every-thing is possible, which is why for the last five years my life has been a series of exasperating and ridiculous failures. Of course that hasn't subdued me, and as always I am loaded down with blueprints of castles in the air, which, God knows, are interesting and appropriate. By the way, castles in the air are always appropriate.

I have only a very tenuous link with *The Contemporary*[27] and took no part in composing its "manifestoes," note that!

As you see I'm publishing too. My hand will dry out my pen from writing.

Keep well, be good! All best wishes. I embrace you and am expecting a letter.

A. Peshkov

87

[*Finland, October 12, 1911*][28]

Aleksei!

Wrote you a long letter . . . and decided not to send it. Really, it's not worth it. Considering the profound alienation and misunderstanding that inspired each word of your letter, my just reproaches won't reach your heart and will only pour oil on the fire. Personal considerations must not force us to part.

The only thing worthy of attention in your letter was your unfavorable reaction to "Darkness"[29] and "My Notes."[30] In this you are really dealing with me (and not with something you have imagined), and to the extent that your rejection is serious and justified, obstacles to friendly cooperation could occur in the very core of our work.

Now I'm finishing a novel, *Sashka Zhegulëv*, and as soon as it comes out I'll send it to you. This work, I think, could help to clarify finally our relations as writers and comrades. You may accept it, and I'll be very glad, but you may reject it and then there'll be nothing to discuss.

For my part I remain your friend, as I wrote you, and I love you. Even if this love has become only pain, that doesn't make it any less.

Your Leonid

12 *October*, 1911, *Terioki*

88

[*Capri, November 3, 1911 (N.S.)*][31]

"Each word in your letter exudes deep alienation and mis-understanding," so you write, Leonid. My dear friend—

115

"alienation" is something I don't feel, and, excuse me for saying so, but you don't either.

If it were otherwise, that is if you believed or I felt this alienation, all dreams of "friendly work together" would be a lie. That's clear.

"Misunderstanding" perhaps is closer to the truth, and you ought to have sent me the letter with "reproaches," even if they had reached my heart. Surely I love you with my heart, not with my head.

I'm eagerly waiting for your story,[32] with great impatience.

Oh Lord, how disgusting this racket by dead souls about *The Living Corpse*[33] is and how shamelessly they all express their complete lack of respect for Tolstoy in public and especially in the press!

I am very tired of these attacks of madness, which are getting me down more and more.

Keep well, I press your hand.

A. Pesh

89

[Finland (?), late 1911-early 1912][34]

You know, my dear Alekseiushka, what the tragedy of our relationship is: you have never and never will let me be frank with you. You are strange; I know you do not like asceticism, but at the same time you are an ascetic; I have never met a man who would so obstinately or so cruelly mortify his personal life, his personal conversation, his personal sufferings. I lived on Capri almost side by side with you for almost half a year, I underwent almost unbearable and dangerous storms and stresses, I was seeking sympathy and advice, especially in my personal life, which was in a crisis, and you and I talked only about literature and social problems. This is a fact: while I was living alongside you, I was waiting for the arrival of Veresaev[35] to consult with him as to whether to end my relationship with you or not.

How can you cut the soul off from the body? I don't live by ideas alone, my personal life is as much of a fact as my literature;

how can one divide one from another and say to one's personal life: do not exist, pretend that you are not here, go hide? One way or another, all that I write, think, and feel is the result of my personal experience. But good Lord, you yourself read biographies and know why this is necessary, but you have walled yourself off from my biography as your neighbor and comrade. And you have walled yourself in as if you too were not a man. Yes, side by side, but like two books on the library shelf; and it has proved so easy to divide us: just stretch out your hand and set one aside.

And as a result there are so many misunderstandings, grievous misunderstandings, cruel injustices. And such purposeless and unnecessary solitude, such voluntary seclusion in a hermitage under a pine tree.

If only I did not love you. But I really love you, in human and not in literary terms, and we did nothing more offensive and senseless than keeping silent about ourselves. I even chattered about myself on the sly, between the lines, what I could, and only kept quiet about you. And I kept silent about your works too; then I would have had to touch on your personal life, on you yourself, and this was not allowed.

I am planting trees, I have built a house, children have been born, I have a wife, acquaintances, various contacts, and I have to be silent about all this. And if I have used the wrong word in a story I can consult with you and you will help with pleasure, but if a difficulty should arise in my life, and my writing itself may depend on it, still I can't talk of it or ask advice, I mustn't, it is bad. But why is it bad? Only by friendship with people, by consulting them and having faith in them can we construct a good life, correct our errors, without prolonging them until they become crimes.

There are a lot of beasts among people, and this prevents correct relationships. But if you do not pay attention to the beasts and don't take into account the beast's bellowing and its vile, fantastic, subhuman imitations (and this is possible), one may be confident and frank in public, in front of everyone. I am an individualist, true, but now for example I am thinking up an essay (and I have thought about it for many years) on several secular ceremonies for unbelievers: birth, marriage, death, and a funeral. And in these ceremonies of mine the people play the main role: they are the godfather and in their presence the newborn baby is named and put under their protection, and before them he takes his vows; the people are also the father who gives the bride away, and the couple is accountable to them. And I would have divorce made public; they may divorce, but they must be accountable to the people and if they do not wish or cannot reveal what is completely secret, let them just declare: we are divorcing.

And I assign such a place to the people because I feel my vital brotherhood and sonship with it, and my conscience is nothing but an eternal answer to the people. Now I would not confess myself to the people; I am frightened by the large number of beasts, but I would make my confession to individuals, and this is neither garrulousness nor displaying my scabs nor lack of self-respect, but a feeling of brotherhood which joins me, an individualist, with all the world.

Oh my Lord, how many slaps I have received from this frankness, how many times my soul has been spat on and my words and meaning distorted; the time is such that if you go to the public square to repent you are called a self-advertiser and they not only label you that but it turns out to be an advertisement. And how many times have I solemnly sworn to be as silent in the presence of every man as I would be with a gendarme at an investigation, and each time I spill over.

Understand how hard it was for me to be silent with you, because it was completely unnatural. And is it possible that that is the way it will be in the future, and again such misunderstandings as those in your recent letter will be possible, and sitting proudly apart behind iron doors we shall call to each other across the street just to edify the passers by?

I am working like a *Wunderkind* and I still cannot plunge into writing letters. The trouble is that I want to write a lot. But I shall continue what I have begun.

My dear odd fellow, why did you take it upon yourself to judge my life from within—you don't know anything about it. You noted everything, but did you observe that for two years I have written nine signatures in all, in other words nothing? For, to put it briefly, beside that misfortune which you forgot about and which could in itself ruin a man, the death of Shura[36], I have undergone a misfortune even greater (this you do not know), of so serious a nature that I consider my two-year illness a cheap payment; another in my place, less strong, would simply have gone mad. It is just this year that I have begun to get better and come to myself.

After your second letter I felt that you still love me a little and had lost all desire to take into consideration, to worry about details, to explain and demonstrate, but my desire to talk with you in straightforward and friendly fashion, concealing nothing personal, is all the greater. It seems to me that this could only be a pleasure for you and for me, and many things will appear in a different light. It would please me, at any rate; I have long been feeling "a hunger for people."

Life is so disturbing that I fear that I shall never finish the letter. I shall send it this way. Forgive the typewriter and the pencil; suddenly the writer does not have a single pen in his house.

Did you receive *Zhegulëv*?[37] I sent it in galley proofs; tomorrow perhaps I shall send some more. *Zhegulëv* was published at a rotten time; Izmailov[38] immediately enclosed it in his froglike embraces and no good things come to Sashka; the police did not kill him but the critics are beating him to death. But I am not at all disconsolate and am even very gay.

I kiss you. I shall write in a few days.

Your Leonid

90

[*Capri, late 1911-early 1912*][39]

"You have never allowed and do not now permit anyone to be frank with you," you write. I think that's not true; for sixteen years and to this day I have been living as a receptacle for others' secrets and thoughts, as if some unseen finger had inscribed on my brow: "Trash heap here." Oh, how much I know and how hard it is to forget!

I have never permitted anyone to touch on my personal life and don't intend to. I am I, and it is no one's business what is wrong with me, if something is wrong with me. To display your scabs to the world, to rub them in public and be bathed in pus, to spatter the eyes of others with your bile, as many do (and as our evil genius Fëdor Dostoevsky did most repulsively of all) —this is a base business, and harmful, of course.

We shall all die, and the world will continue to live. It has shown to me and attached to me much that is evil and filthy, but I do not want and will not accept its loathsomeness. I have and shall continue to take from the world its good aspects, I have nothing to avenge myself for, no reason to embitter others by a disgraceful display of my wounds and sores or to deafen them with my screeches.

"Brotherhood" does not at all mean (as it is understood among us) showing your brother your inner vileness and dirt, but in keeping silence in shame about this if you cannot eliminate it.

The writer of our day has become especially repulsive recently by walking in public without his pants hind-end-first and mournfully displaying to the world the place that hurts, and this place hurts him because he does not know where he can sit down peacefully.

"Why did you take it upon yourself to judge my life," you write. I did not judge your life, I spoke about your literary work, spoke and *did not judge*. In general, I don't judge, I say what I like and what I don't.

A book, I think, is more harmful or more useful than a man, and this is why: a book lives longer than a man in the world, and for me, a man of this world, a book is more interesting than the head that created it; I say the head because nowadays no one can write about the heart. The world is supported by activity, and the longer it lasts the more fulfilled it becomes, and the man who has asserted a passive attitude toward the world, whoever he may be, is my enemy, since I have asserted that one's attitude toward life and mankind must be active. In this I am a fanatic. Many, allured by the corrupt chatter of the Asiatic and nihilist Ivan Karamazov, preach, most vulgarly, about "nonacceptance" of the world, in view of its "cruelty" and "senselessness." Were I Governor General, I wouldn't hang revolutionists, but these same "nonaccepters," for these tongue-lechers are more harmful for our country than plague rats.

I read *Sashka*.[40] It is badly written, dull and uneven. To my mind only Sashka's sister was successful; she was the only one you described without clever intellectualizing, and she turned out wonderfully. But Sashka himself is a wooden blockhead, who has long been known to us; it is still that same "lamb" which has been chewed up by Russian literature, *i.e.,* a ram who offers himself as a sacrifice for "the sins of the world," placing on himself a load which cannot be comfortably borne and groaning in various voices but always in the same way, in our decade as in the eighties, under his own yoke, which he has allegedly shouldered of his own free will.

But it was not at all voluntary and always beyond his strength— never for himself but necessarily in the name of something.

In general, you have become too literary, in the sense that your inspirations are cold and calculated. You are deceiving yourself when you say that "all that I write, think, and feel is the result of my personal experience." Let's leave aside "think" and "feel," they have no place in this sentence, but you won't insist, surely, that *Sashka* is the result of your "personal experience," since, although this story is stuffed with facts about Russian reality, the exposition and interpretation of the facts are completely literary, *i.e.,* artificial, not alive. Now if you had gotten indictments from lawyers who worked on expropriation cases, let's say in the Urals, or even better, investigation proceedings, and had read them well, then you really might talk about "personal experience." From these documents you would have seen how unnatural the whole situation of Sashka's life was and how superfluous the Gnedois were. There is a person who is living with me now who has known Savitskii from high school and has kept up with his activity; of course, personal evidence is not worth much since it is subjective, but just the same you must treat reality more seriously than you have allowed yourself to.

They should send you to Viatka[41] so that you could float out of the "ocean" of your cold intellectualities, and when you struck the rock of reality you would howl and roar like a human being!

You and I have drawn apart, and will draw apart still further, not because personal relations did not arise between us but because they could not. It seemed to us that they were possible, but we were wrong. We are too different. I am a man on the sidelines and live on the sidelines and I am not an intellectual—God save me! Yes, it is terribly sad that there is no more Lady Shura;[42]—what a wonderful creature she was, I love her, I see clearly to this day her eyes, her smile, her irregular teeth—how terribly fine it was that they were irregular.

And in your work everything is strictly correct, everything is ruled, and therefore everything is dull.

Don't think that I consider myself a surgeon of morals and think that it is possible to cut out of a man what he was born with: of course not: if you have a snub nose, that's the way you'll die.

Each of us keeps the same nose that nature has given him, only one need not proclaim so insistently: my olfactory organ is the most sensitive and beautiful in the world, since it smells everywhere the stink of decay!

Keep well,[43] grow big, don't get angry with me—it's no use. And there's no reason, my feelings for you are very good, I know that.

Good-bye,
A. Pesh . . .

91

[Finland, March 28, 1912][44]

For a long time I couldn't decide whether to answer your letter or be silent, and by silence, without unnecessary conversation, put a cross on our relations. I knew that my letter would be painful for you in one way or another, and I have never wanted to add another drop of bitterness to the life which you must lead far away from your native land and your dear ones and which in itself is not sweet. But on the other hand I feared and still fear that my silence would be incorrectly interpreted and like all other incorrect interpretations will harm you again. Finally, neither of us is so weak, however our lives have turned out, that we lack enough strength both to express and to listen to the most difficult matters. That's why I'm writing.

I'll begin by pointing out that all my letters have been gentle, correct, and did not transgress by a single coarse word the limits of conversation or dispute which are the only ones possible for self-respecting people. Of course I don't at all approve of everything in your life (not your personal life, of course), but I didn't think I was justified in judging you without knowing all the facts; and my letters don't contain a single word of accusation or reproach. And when I mentioned a lack of frankness on your part and ours in my last letter, I put it in a general way and offered it for discussion, like a question.

But your letters (except for the short second one) were impermissibly and causelessly coarse, sometimes approaching street swearing in character, causelessly malicious and smugly unjust. I would even call them cynical, they were so coarse and gave so little evidence of any respect for your own words and for mankind generally. Even if you have no reason to respect me, that doesn't relieve you of the obligation to be polite and self-contained and not to judge categorically and peremptorily about matters of which you know nothing. But I'll speak later of your lack of respect for people.

The idea behind your first letter was that in my drive for glory (this is your favorite thought, which you also express in print) I have begun to write bad works, that my life is such that I am not only bad myself but set a bad example to others, as I'm almost the source and in any case a sponsor and encourager of all that is loathsome in modern literary circles. The cynic Kuprin,[45] a friend of the *Petersburg Gazette*[46] and the *Blue Journal*,[47] you placed alongside me, actually even a bit behind me. And you said all this, not so much as if you were fully convinced but rather as if it were a fact and an objective truth, as if you knew not only everything obvious but everything secret too, even to the motive of my actions, which has been concealed from everyone else: a love of glory. Living a thousand versts away from us, even apparently forgetting what I look like, on the basis of newspapers and hearsay slander, the articles of Merezhkovskii[48] and the "carter rabble," you have passed on me a sentence which, by its decisiveness, its brevity and infraction of all the norms of justice, recalls the sentences of Russian courts-martial. Like a tragic abnormality, even exceeding the bounds of the courts-martial, you added at the end of your letter the declaration that all my attempts to justify myself would be useless. In other words, you not only did not hear the accused before passing sentence but refused beforehand to hear him. Even the all-knowing God does not act in this way, even he at one time listened to Makar.[49]

You haven't accused me of a trifle but of the most important crime which can exist for a writer: venality. For what is the drive for glory which could make a writer write badly? Isn't it the same as what a man sells himself for: money, women, glory, or a bottle of vodka? A writer may be so accused only with the greatest care, when one has at hand genuine facts; otherwise, this accusation does not differ in any way from the ordinary shrill slander which the uncultured, envious, and pathetic newspaper riff-raff engage in for mutual amusement. What facts do you have? Facts so undisputable and convincing that my own words would be unnecessary? When and with what even did this drive for glory, this venality, begin?

There is one almost infallible sign by which we may know a venal writer: he writes not for himself but for a master, whoever he may be: the government, the public, the crowd. That is the whole nature of the *New Times*[50] and the "new timers"; at most they only change their masters, but the servile attitude is retained in everything. I remember how you analyzed the first issue of Amfiteatrov's[51] *Red Banner* and found in it the servile features of the new timers.

But which of my works, and for what master were they written? And what reward did I have for my servility? *King Hunger*,[52] which I told you about in Capri and for which the whole press attacked me, both the rightists and the leftists? "The Seven Who Were Hanged"[53]—that story was successful, that's true, but if I was a lackey in this I waited on the same table as Tolstoy, who was writing "I Cannot Be Silent" at the same time? *Black Maskers*,[54] "My Notes,"[55] "Darkness"[56]—all works generously abused, from the right and from the left, and giving no one the type of pleasure for which a servile lackey is paid? On the whole it is a fruitless activity to list my writings; in none of them, whatever the subject matter, can be found even a hint of servility, of a desire to skim the top of dominant tastes and moods. Would you take *The Ocean*,[57] which all the Izmailovs[58] are still scoffing at? or *Sashka Zhegulëv*,[59] which united Zinaida Hippius[60] and Maxim Gorky, Izmailov, and Red'ko,[61] in a common attack? The censorship cuts me, the critics slander me, I have no haven in a single literary group, I haven't a single friend in the whole press—such are the fruits of my drive for glory.

In your last letter you expressed your thoughts on this matter even more specifically: that I, in your own words, participated in the dances on the graves. Just when and where did I dance? In "The Seven Who Were Hanged," or *Sashka Zhegulëv*? And you make such accusations without the least self-doubt, you reinforce it with your respectable signature, and consider it so immutable that anything I might say on this subject would be "useless." And I have only one thing I can say: you, Maxim Gorky, respect neither mankind in general nor the writer, just as they are not respected by courts-martial and all others who accuse a man of vileness with a light heart.

There is one almost infallible sign by which we may know the man who does not respect other people: that is the ease with which he slanders, besmirches, and condemns a man. Respect rests on the presumption that a man is good and that the reverse must be proven. And the contrary would be that a man would be presumed capable of any sort of meanness, and, whatever might be said of him, whatever he may be accused of, all is easily and cheaply believed. In its further development this leads to a search for the vilest motives behind all of man's actions: if he lives that way it is for renown; if he writes it is for money or glory, if he groans it is to get sympathy, if he is well it is to boast and because he is a fool. Specifically, a Russian characteristic, which once you experienced directed at yourself, and now, at a distance and knowing nothing, you direct at me.

But in your attitude toward mankind there is something else which is no less striking than lack of respect: it is arrogance. There is no other word which I can use to describe your tone: on the one hand, scorn, on the other, superiority, which you use in your explanations and accusations. With a completely arrogant gesture you distribute your cuffs, you condemn, you reprieve, without even requiring an explanation from the slave; it doesn't even enter your head that through the majesty of your pose may be seen that very "Asiaticism" which you cannot find words to stigmatize sufficiently. Such you used not to be, Maxim Gorky, and I have little faith now in your democratic convictions.

When I speak of my own affairs I do not at all expect to justify myself; I am only pointing out the malicious unproved slander which accompanies your severe accusations. But beside my works, you, with the same know-it-all and peremptory tone, have condemned my life; where have you learned about my life? You are a blind and conceited man; you know nothing and understand very little and your judgments are oversimplified and you have unlimited faith in them. Or is your knowledge based on what is printed about me in the papers?

Here I must admit that there is one fact which supports your accusations. That is my telegram to Iasinskii.[62] But in pronouncing sentence on me for this occurrence, you should have first asked me *why I did this*, and then find out whether this fact is not such an exception that generalizations on the basis of it cannot be justified. And actually this fact is *exceptional*, and all the other facts confirm this sufficiently. Did you know that I have taken part in other "celebrations" of that type and in general in all types of celebrations? Did you know why I refused to participate in the Tolstoy evening? Did you know that I, apparently alone among all our writers, sent a refusal on principle to participate in the Gogol celebration, and what my motives were? As an exhibit I am sending you a copy of my letter to Gruzinskii.[63] Did you know the facts about my participation in a disreputable journal, cooperating with disreputable men? Did you know that at my own demand *Pale Horse*[64] was thrown out of *Shipovnik* and that for this Filosofov[65] honored me with an article on "Delusions of Grandeur"? Did you know that at present I have armed all the brethren of the streets against myself, the Arabazhins,[66] the Izmailovs, and so on?

Judge yourself how insignificant the matter with Iasinskii (the reasons for such an action you don't know) is beside other matters which I refuse to name more in detail; I haven't the time or the desire.

Such was your first letter. Well, of course I didn't think it was even possible to answer that one, it was so bad. But in the second you admitted that you don't completely understand me. And that was enough for me to cancel your previous letter: even if we assume, I thought, that he could understand me, it would not be worth while to climb up the wall because of the expressions and the tone he used when so much serious work lies ahead. And with my same old unfortunate faith in mankind I wrote you a second friendly letter, which I didn't even have time to finish, unfortunately, and I get back a completely unexpected, wildly coarse and frenzied answer. I admit I don't understand even now its intentional sharpness, its desire to offend at all cost —even to the extent of clumsily and ridiculously asserting that "Everything about you is correct, everything is ruled, and therefore everything is dull."

The whole letter from beginning to end is incredible; I'll only stop to point out how wildly and distortedly you interpreted my words on frankness. You begin by asserting that all your life you have been a "trash heap," which you assumed included my frankness. I don't know how much others have heaped trash on you—it is not true of me, and I pointed that out in my letter. Further on, the same arrogant gesture: "I have never permitted anyone to touch on my personal life and don't intend to." But that's not only arrogance, it's hysteria, a screech. One might think that I, like the most complete boor, am crawling into your life and you are sharply repulsing me. On your conscience, have I ever made any such attempt? Then why this sense of injury? And further on, how distortedly and onesidedly you interpreted the very concept of frankness. "To display your scabs to the world, to rub them in public and be bathed in pus, to spatter the eyes of others with your bile, as many do (and as our evil genius Fëdor Dostoevsky did most repulsively of all)— this is a base business, and harmful, of course."

So you apparently supposed that I wanted to bestow on you my pus and bile and that in general there can be no other matter for frankness aside from pus, bile, and trash? What a wonderful opinion you have of a man who respects you. And suddenly I wanted to consult with you about my life and its direction, the same life about which you yourself have only just written, "They should send you to Viatka." And what's this about "Fëdor Dostoevsky," who of course needs no defense and whom you tossed with one stroke into the same pile with Tolstoy, who wrote *My Confession*, with Rousseau, and with quite a few others; actually there isn't a writer who either directly or indirectly has not spoken of his personal life or of his own sufferings and joys. Isn't that what you're talking about? And if it is one man's hind-end that hurts, in your expression, in others it is their human soul that hurts, and this pain is the ornament and justification of life; why do you see only the hind-end of a respected man and substitute it for the soul?

Finally the last important point in your letter, the essence: "You and I have drawn apart, and will draw apart still further, not because personal relations did not arise between us but because they could not. It seemed to us that they were possible, but we were wrong. We are too different."

No, Aleksei, that's not true; you and I were not so different. Remember better and think a bit. We only became different when you changed your views and tastes and I became an "*anarchist*" to you in the abusive and shameful sense. There was a time when you had another attitude toward anarchism; and still not so long ago that same Judas Iscariot,[67] whom you attack me in *Russian Word*[68] for defending (thus sharing the views of Arabazhin and the Black Hundred newspapers), you once valued very highly, and you yourself helped me in the work and published "Judas" in your *Znanie*. And also a very short time ago you would have had a completely different concept of "Darkness" and "My Notes" and would not have stretched out a hand to Merezhkovskii (*and not for the first time*) in interpreting these stories as reactionary. You yourself changed sharply, Aleksei, and that's the cause of our parting, and perhaps the source of all your coarse and baseless accusations.

(Note) By the way, you remember why on returning from Capri to Russia I refused to edit the *Znanie* volume? I wanted to invite Blok[69] and Sologub,[70] but you opposed this and were impossibly hostile in your attacks on both of them. Now Blok is in *Znanie*. I could point out still other inconsistencies, the reasons for which lie in a change, but not in me.

Both your understanding and apparently your character have changed. You wrote everything with the same lack of self-understanding: "I live in Russia more than you"—this is a bitter error (I say nothing about the comparison, and I don't know why you made it). You live in Capri, and neither the mass of letters nor those individual examples of Russians whom you meet bring you closer to Russia. When the German goes to the zoo and sees a Bengal tiger there, that still does not mean that he has been to India. And however many tigers you have seen, you are far from Russia. You must smell the air yourself, you must see the crowd on the street, you must enter into the stream of all these little Russian matters, and faces, and fellows, to feel the real thing . . . but what's the use of talking. And I'm sure that if fate had been less senselessly cruel to you and had permitted you to live in present-day Russia, you would think differently.

A sad indication of your remoteness from Russia, to my mind, is your article in *Russian Word;* it has all the features of an intellectual weeping in repentance, and an intellectual in the pure sense is the man most remote from Russia, as you know. Without sensing it yourself, in a cruel, unjust, and unfounded condemnation of "Great Russia," you approach the position of the contributors to the volume *Landmarks,*[71] even Rodionov's[72] position. You curse that very sectarianism which even in its most monstrous forms among the people always expressed only the will for creativity and freedom, undimmed rebellion; you consider the Great Russian capable only of "evasions of life," naïvely forgetting who then has created this ugly but immense and terribly strong state, Russia. If the Great Russian only avoids life, who then suppresses the Finns, the Poles, the Ukrainians, shoves out in all directions even in times of disconsolation like the present, usually conducts actual looting in Persia and wherever else it may? Speak of the barbaric quality, the lack of culture, the historic backwardness of the people, but do not speak of weakness and passivity of those who so actually, although rudely, create an immense state, which may only be accused of cruelty, not of the gentleness of the eternal slobberer.

For convenience you have also admitted our literature to be a matter of chance, as if *chance* were possible here, as if you yourself had not spoken a few lines back of the unalterable "laws of history." *The West has distorted your view by the instruments of its own struggle, and you have ceased to understand that our instruments for the struggle are entirely different,* and that our evil genius Dostoevsky is actually a rebel, a teacher of action, and that he taught you rebellion. The glossy bourgeoisie of the West, like every bourgeoisie, falls to ashes in Dostoevsky's presence, and this is the most genuine and the most permanent revolution.

Instead of looking at tigers, you should look at the Moscow carthorse, and the darkness would fall from your eyes and, as before, when you were on the Volga, you would understand that the works of the Great Russians are not at all bad and that there is no need to fear for their fate. Perhaps now you will suspect me of nationalism?—that would be unjust.

It was very unpleasant that in the article "On the Present Day" you did not name me directly when you spoke of attempts to justify Judas. Russian literature is not so expansive that one cannot guess what is being discussed, and a direct accusation would be more pleasant in all respects. By the way, I too wanted to oppose you in an article; but after thinking it over I decided that it would be harmful for our work. I lose nothing by refraining, and if I begin to object, our street will relish the scandal and won't get the point. Especially since in general your condemnation of contemporary writers is just and it would not be in the general interest to weaken its significance.

If, with all that you have written about me, you have found it possible to end your last letter with the words: "my feelings for you are very good, I know that," then I can say this with still more justification. My love for you was too strong for even you to destroy it so easily and at once. And whatever you said and however offensively I think you have erred, I know your impartiality, and there are no terrible errors while it is present, although there may be *fatal* errors.

If I give you pain with this letter, forgive me. I have not written it for that reason at all. In spite of reason, in spite of passion, I continue to feel that an unbreakable bond unites us, which cannot be destroyed even by your will. And I am sure that if we can *talk* together (and not write), at least for a few hours, many misunderstandings would disappear. You have forgotten me, friend.

With all my soul I wish you well, with all my heart.

L. A.

March 28, 1912

92

[*Capri, April* 24, 1912 (*N.S.*)][73]

It is not true, Leonid, that my letters to you are malicious, cynical, etc.; there is nothing like that in them and cannot be.

All that was said in the second letter about "frankness" is general in character and not directed against you, but against our vile characteristics; the words "to display your scabs to the world,"[74] etc., were not written for you; Barbara in *The Summer Folk*[75] spoke them, and since then I have repeated them at least ten times, I even repeated them in the article "On the Present Day."[76]

Please understand that the "frankness" which I have in mind is that of boasting about one's personal torments, boasting which has flooded Russian literature. It has an ascetic character, and is darkening our lives. It comes from our Christianity and has such apologists among us as Tolstoy, Dostoevsky, Solov'ëv,[77] and—now—Rozanov.[78] It is infecting us.

As for the cult of Judas,[79] I could not have had you in mind; I am very sorry that I did not clarify it and quoted Roslavlev,[80] forgetting Pavel Popov,[81] Golovanov,[82] and others touching on this theme.* When I talked about it, I was talking about writers of the street and about the way that they vulgarize great ideas. I must still speak on this theme, and I shall take care to make an exception of your Judas, although, to my mind, it of course does not need this.

Blok[83] in *Znanie* is bad as an example of my inconsistency; Blok was published by Piatnitskii[84] and Miroliubov,[85] and I as before see no need of this, but I don't want to be mixed up with it, as my relations with *Znanie* have changed. You could offer as an example of my inconsistency my correspondence with Rozanov; that is something! Or my attitude toward Shaliapin,[86] for which I am abused in many languages.

In general, your letter is strange, raging in a sense, and actually coarse. When I write coarsely, it is simply my way, but that is not at all your character. It seems to me that you did not get angry with my letters but with my article "On the Present Day," which you read very badly and with prejudice.

Even if I admit that my letters have hurt you to some extent, your last letter has more than paid me back for all the "offenses" which I have supposedly committed against you—an amazingly clumsy letter.

It is very annoying that you wrote in such a strange tone; it ties my hands and confuses my relationship with you. If our correspondence is not to stop, I shall have to "select my expressions" in my letters to you, which I cannot bear. It seemed to me that your attitude toward me was more sincere and simple and that such immense misunderstandings as the present were impossible.

I remind you of what was said in one of the letters: "I did not judge your life, I spoke of your literature, spoke and did not judge." I only mentioned Iasinskii[87] because your intimacy with him might be interpreted hostilely for you, since you had already aroused too hostile and unjust an attitude toward yourself,[88] as I see no less clearly than you do.

I think that we must temporarily stop corresponding, so that this offensive misunderstanding can settle down; I cannot consider myself the only guilty party, as you, I think, will agree.

Keep well, I press your hand.

A. Peshkov

April, 24, 1912

* There are now more than ten original and translated Judases in Russian literature. Soon Vessel's tetralogy will come out on this theme; that will be candy for the streets!

93

[Finland, April 8, 1912][89]

As you so justly noted, Aleksei, it is not in my nature to be coarse; and it is even less in my nature to give way to unprovoked rage. And, in fact, very important and serious reasons were necessary to make me write so angry a letter (I still don't think it coarse or enraged). You assume that the real reason for my hurt feelings was your article; no, that is not true at all and it only demonstrates that you did not pay proper attention to my letter and have not yet clearly understood the position you took in your previous letters.

The real reason for my resentment was precisely what I wrote you about and it is not worth repeating. And even before the publication of your article I wrote you an angry letter and only delayed in sending it while I struggled with my own perplexity and reluctance to do anything unpleasant to you. I just didn't like your article, and the indirect allusion to my Judas[90] rather hurt me (I am very glad that this was not justified, but others too made the mistake and thought that I was the one you had in mind). And I have already written exactly what I did not like, and I also added that I agree with a great deal in your article.

You think we should stop corresponding for a while? I don't know, perhaps so, but perhaps not. It all depends on how willingly and how seriously we approach this correspondence. I have no doubt that if we could meet and talk with one another we would reach a quick agreement, without catastrophes and misunderstandings. But the same is possible in letters too; surely we are not writers for nothing, and it would be strange and incomprehensible if we could not acquire for our correspondence either the proper manner of expression or language or ability to express ourselves logically and precisely. Your last letter was written with great restraint and seems to confirm my idea; if it were not so short and consequently lacking in specific examples, it might have brought us considerably closer to mutual understanding.

Of course it is hard for men like us to conduct such a correspondence when there is so much work to do, and here again the question is how serious and important our estrangement is for us. If it is of only personal importance, then it is not even worth wasting thought, let alone letters, on it: so they misunderstood each other, so they parted, so this is no uncommon unpleasantness in life.

But if you take into account (as I wrote you earlier) the fact that each of us represents a significant social force, that our friendship or hostility exceeds the bounds of our personal pleasure or annoyance, then of course the labor of corresponding will not seem so fruitless and unnecessary.

I leave it to you to decide this question finally. For my part I think that we ought to come to an understanding and if this cannot be done in person for the present, then it must be done for the present by correspondence. But I repeat, this depends completely on you, and if it is difficult or unpleasant for you to write me, or if it seems unnecessary, then let's drop it, either temporarily or forever.

And if we go on corresponding there is absolutely no need to return to the past and analyze our relations; it is too easy to get confused doing that. It is quite enough if we frankly and directly point out to each other our sins and errors as writers and clarify what our disagreements as writers are. And as long as you speak about my works without suspecting my motives, you can speak as sharply as you want, call me an idiot or whatever you like, and I will never be offended. And even more: if in my work itself (in its tenor or inner construction) you find anything dishonest, bad, amoral, or antisocial, then curse as much as you like and I'll be a fool if I am in the least offended. Understand what hurts me, Aleksei: your doubt, or rather your certainty, of the dishonesty and the impurity of my motives.

And I shall be glad to argue with you and justify myself about "Darkness"[91] and "My Notes"[92] too, and I hope that I shall shake your conviction. And if you let me write you as directly as that, it would be good.

If you decide to stop corresponding either temporarily or completely, then just leave this letter unanswered and I shall understand.

I think we feel the same about Shaliapin;[93] you, too, simply love him, and your kindness to him does not seem to me inconsistent or shameful. As for Rozanov,[94] yes, I was amazed when I read about his boasting about your letters, although I think this rascal boasted about insults. But I still do not understand why you are willing to spend time and labor even to insult this trifling, dirty, repulsive man. There are such mangy dogs, hopelessly doomed to brutishness, which you don't even want to throw stones at, you are sorry for the clean stone.

Next winter in November I am expecting to go to Italy; maybe we can see each other, if we don't go on writing? *My faith in logic and reason is so great*[95] that I cannot think of our relations as hopeless.

I embrace you and warmly press your hand.   *L. A.*

April, 18 1912

94

[*Capri, Spring,* 1912][96]

No, Leonid, I am sure that correspondence will only confuse our relations still more; we look at everything in the world too differently; each of your letters arouses in me a whole stream of objections; if I put them in short sentences they would take on the character of dogmas.

Let's put off quarreling until we meet personally, that's better.

I am sending you a letter, which I received with the request to forward it to you.

Too bad about Strindberg;[97] he was a wonderful rebel.[98]

Keep well, and don't think that my refusal to continue the correspondence comes from any unfriendly feelings. No, I am simply sure that letters will not achieve their purpose.

Best wishes,

A. Pesh . . .

Won't you send me the magazine *Styles and the Gentleman,*[99] the issue in which Batiushkov and the idiot Anichkov teach the Russians how they must wear their trousers? Curious!

But—what have we come to!

95

[*Finland* (?), *Summer,* 1912][1]

Perhaps you are right, Aleksei, and it would be better for us to talk than to write one another. If you are not opposed (you and Mar'ia Fëdorovna,[2] of course) I might come to visit you in Capri in November. But only if you will not feel the least dissatisfaction and if it will not put any of us in an awkward position. For myself I may say that I love you sincerely and the way I used to; however strange it may be, all our correspondence has not left in me the least trace of hostility or irritation. It is too obvious that this is a complete misunderstanding. While I would not force myself on you as a disciple of yours, I think that essentially we think in the same way, more than ever before. You do not yet see this, but time will show.

Today I shall order you *Styles and the Gentleman*.[3] Of course Batiushkov would be a splendid tailor from the Nevskii Prospect, and he buries his talents in literature to no avail. And he is not the only one. What a captivating and talented manager of a house of pleasure Kamenskii[4] would make! The *New Times*[5] as a whole might be moved over to the Donon,[6] and no other restaurant would have such talented and quickfooted waiters. These gentlemen raise the question of dress to a matter of principle; this is funny and sad. But where are they to apply their talents and their restless public spirit?

The first issue of *Legacy*[7] made a good impression, unlike *The Contemporary*,[8] which has been shrill and empty from the beginning. I personally, as a native of Orël, was very flattered by your story; you may not agree, but I think that I am that very "restless son of Orël,"[9] who was born in the steppe with your help. The only thing I didn't like was Ropshin;[10] perhaps because Hippius[11] was not on his back, he was paler than a pale horse and he keeps galloping in the same direction, only with large detours, like a chessboard knight. And his quarrel with Izgoev[12] is silly. I find this bombastic penitent with his sour belches repulsive. I prefer the cheapest little romance to his Lenten truth, which contains not the least grain of truth, like every drunken headache. I. Vol'nyi[13] is very good; who is he?

Here is the trouble: almost all Russian books, novels, and stories now are dull. Not that they are without talent or that they are obvious backward walkers, but somehow dull. Everything is correct, and justified, and the writer is a good fellow, but that is no consolation. Probably my *Zhegulëv*[14] has the same problem. Merezhkovskii[15] is unbearable, Briusov[16] is dull to the point of madness; if you take up a volume of young writers, you are bored with it—bears and lame masters and swine, and all to no purpose. Each person writes precisely and asks himself: and is it all right for me to describe a sunset? Perhaps sunsets ought not to be described nowadays. And it is also possible that there is no sunset, so I shall describe a little semi-sunset.

I have not begun to write about Strindberg. It is late and I know little about him, he never made much of an impression on me, and I have not thought about him. It is not worth while volunteering such an "opinion" as this.

And now, Aleksei, tell me your opinion. Razumnik[17] and I (mainly I, but I put it that way for propriety) have decided to put out a volume for the benefit of the Lena workers,[18] cheap; it would not cost more than half a ruble. Korolenko[19] has promised to help, no one prejudiced or even indifferent will participate, and we are trying to keep it as clean and sincere as possible. Would you like to contribute a story or an article? Although V. E. Kopel'man[20] will work on the material, the *Shipovnik* firm will not issue it.

Probably you receive all the books, but if you need anything write and I shall send it.

As your friend I warmly press your hand.

Leonid Andreev

96

[*Capri, Summer, 1912*][21]

I'm sure that when we meet there won't be any "awkward situation," but that it will be a fine reunion of two comrades who have not seen each other for a long time.

Vol'nyi[22]—be proud!—is an Orël boy, extraordinarily nice, intelligent, and, it seems to me, talented.

What—Ropshin![23] Read Vinnichenko;[24] that will console you even more.

Some sort of new—strange—streak of portraiture has begun in Russian literature: Sholom Asch[25] has just published a story depicting Volynskii,[26] Chirikov,[27] Dymov,[28] Burdes,[29] and Khodotov[30] and a whole slew of others very boorishly. Recently I read a manuscript devoted to Artsybashev,[31] I have a very vile story about Kuprin,[32] Old Man Teternikov[33] has scrawled about me, Dymov, and, as they say, Merezhkovskii,[34] and Ropshin also makes little portraits. What does this mean?

The volume for the benefit of the Lena strikers,[35] of course, won't succeed, and you shouldn't have taken it on. When do you expect to bring it out? Tell me and maybe I'll have time and will send a manuscript. Very busy; some sort of "International League" is being formed—its manifesto will be printed in *Demands of Life*—I'm also mixed up in this thing.

How do you like Surguchev?[36] I just saw him off to Russia yesterday.

Aleksei Zolotarev[37] has written a marvellous thing; you'll see, I'm not exaggerating.

He's living here, Vol'nyi too, and in general it's glorious here.

You were right about Batiushkov:[38] he's a tailor and an old-clothes-man.

I have enough work for forty years, but I don't have time to do anything.

Books? I'd very much like to have Maupassant in the *Shipovnik*[39] edition, but won't Kopel'man send it? Well—it's become expensive to publish books!

What are you doing there—gotten rich from hunger? Send if you can: C. Pearson, *Grammar of Science*.[40] It's also a *Shipovnik* publication.

Well, keep well. All best wishes!

A.

You know, there's an interesting writer in Russia, Zhakov,[41] a Ziranian. A curious character!

97

[Finland,] November 15, 1911 [1912][42]

Dear Aleksei!

Well, I didn't get to Capri, and I don't know whether I shall this winter. I'm kept back by my work, the theaters, and various private matters. I'm very sorry about this, as we ought to get together and talk things over; I keep on believing with the persistence of an idiot that we could get back on the very best terms.

It's very hard to live in Russia now. If in the depths some internal enrichment and growth is taking place, it is at the expense of the top levels: there's dirt and neglect on top. And it's worst of all with us writers. My optimism of last year got me in a mess. Strange as it may seem, only the modernists live well and freely; on the whole they have gathered strong forces, gotten on the newspapers, and are penetrating the journals. If you'd like I'll write in more detail about how things are with us and them. Of the big and the vilest things in life I don't speak, you know that yourself, and generally, if you'd like, I can make reports to you from time to time, very subjective ones of course.

And how have things turned out with our Ivan Pavlovich?[43] I'm very sorry for him: first the fire and then the crash. He's had bad luck. He almost ruined *Shipovnik*, but it seems to have survived. I nearly parted with it; they've very much distorted a publishing house that had been clean but profitable, and there was absolutely nothing to be done. But I haven't merged with anyone else; I have no haven. For the present my works will be published by Blumenberg. I've gotten rid of Tseitlin;[44] he has the old rights and I have rights to everything new.

Did you receive Maupassant?[45]

Warm embraces.

Your L. A.

Terioki

98

[Capri, late 1912]*[46]*

"The heart does not permit the heart to live." I was just starting to write you an abusive letter about your spat with the Kievans. What's biting you? And so the Ukraine plans to walk out on Russia, and you keep on irritating them, so you're speeding up the disintegration of the Empire.

Of course I haven't received Maupassant,[47] and it would be fine to have "eighteen volumes in luxurious bindings"—I love luxury!

And I'm a poor man, broke; I've nothing to buy books with. I must be given books; I'm an old man, worthy—I have 243 medals, among them many rare ones and one special one: it was stamped in Russia in 905 and it states: "May the Lord raise us in His time."

There's something mystical and deeply trustworthy in this.

Write me about the modernists. I'm very interested. It seems that Viktorian Mirotëkov[48] has gathered them into his "Muir and Merilees"?[49] And you're there with them, did I see? You didn't have to do that, old man, but anyway that's your business. I, an old baldy, don't understand modern games very well, and my weak mind cannot make out how a Shestov[50]-Chernov[51]-Razumnik[52]-Mstislavskii[53] quadrille is possible? And why not proclaim that "in order to meet the confused tastes and obscure demands of the witless Russian public, we have decided to publish our respectable journal in four directions at once—if you please!" Although—returning to you personally—I understand: there's nowhere to write.

It's too bad that you weren't here this summer: a good group turned up and we passed the time happily. We lived in the sea—wonderful!

Send me the play about the professor;[54] it should be interesting. But I didn't like Katerina.[55] There's something blind in her. You half succeed with old women, measuring from the bottom up. You don't see even their maternal breasts—or don't you value that?

You see, I'm already beginning to talk with Rogachevskii's[56] lisping tongue.

So—I'm waiting for Maupassant and letters.

But look, Leonid: a good group has undertaken a worthwhile and necessary job: to organize a museum on the history of Russia's struggle for liberation in the nineteenth century, beginning with Alexander I or even earlier. The Academy of Sciences is doing a similar job in Russia—in part—but that's impossible to do completely, on a broad basis, under our political and social conditions. It has been decided to do the work —for the present—abroad. There are some things, and some will be acquired. We have few means, and we have to pay for the premises, etc. I urge you, give us money! And if you have any documents, letters, books, give us those too.

Send money to Evgenii Aleksandrovich Liatskii,[57] Kamennoostrovskii 65, 31, or to him c/o the editorial offices of *The Contemporary*.

Keep well!

Don't you have some rich friends? Get money from them, as much as they'll give.

It's a very important matter.

I press your hand.

A. P . . .

99

[*Finland (?), December* 26, 1912][58]

Maupassant is on its way.[59]

And you're muttering nonsense, old man. Haven't I sung the praises of the maternal and the good in women in *Stars*[60] and in "Vasilii,"[61] and in "Red Laugh"[62] . . . but in almost everything? "Anfisa"?[63] But I just didn't succeed with her. You don't like "The Seven Who Were Hanged"[64] (and it will do you no good), but you look at my intentions: are the women in that undervalued? and in *Anathema?*[65]

That's how the theater interprets Katerina,[66] as essential purity. And how stirring it was; I roared at the rehearsal like an aqueduct that has burst. This has never happened to me before. God willing you'll see it, and I swear, Aleksei, you'll roar too. By the way Nemirovich[67] and the Muscovites told me how well *The Lower Depths*[68] went last season, a real hit.

And in general you're muttering nonsense. You think I'm "Mirotëkovizing,"[69] but I've been fighting and trading with them for half a year now. The truth is there's nowhere to work, and for a long time now I've just been contributing stories, not *cooperating* in anything. And I keep dreaming, and I keep talking about some journal of my own. I'm weary of living and working and fighting alone—but there's no way out. Who am I? For the nobly born decadents, a despised realist; for the congenital realists, a despised symbolist. Even Zhenichka Chirokiv,[70] now winged with success, teaches me: don't give in to the macaronis, throw away the black masks, write "Once upon a Time"[71] again. And if it's so hard to find a place in the world of art, it's completely hopeless in the world at large. The languages have become confounded.

December 26. Am leaving for Capri tomorrow. Kisses, I'm very glad I'll see you.

Your L.

100

[Finland, 1913 (?)][72]

Dear Aleksei,

We are leaving to go abroad before May and my house is standing empty and uninhabited. Wouldn't it suit you for a living place for a while, until you have made final arrangements? The house is big and will hold all who accompany you and is convenient for living and for working, especially for working. There is a telephone to St. Petersburg, horses, and it is beautiful here and nonintellectual, there are only Finns. There is only one inconvenience: the house must be heated in the frost, but that is a trifle. We could arrange to have the house at your disposal for the summer too; I will be at the fjords in the summer. I would be very glad if this plan should be acceptable and convenient for you.

Answer me or have someone answer me. I will be here until the 14th, and if you agree I will prepare the house for your arrival. The main thing is for you to be comfortable.

Our general personal misunderstandings have nothing to do with this, and you can trust me. I warmly press your hand and wish you all the best.

Your Leonid

Write: Terioki, c/o Vammel's.

101

[1914 (?)][73]

I think the following criticism could be made:

The Book of Judges does not call Samson[74] a prophet; he is only a Nazarite, one who has dedicated himself to God, given a pledge not to taste wine, not to cut his hair, and not to touch a corpse. If he broke this pledge in any way, the Nazarite was obliged to shave his hair. "Strength in his hair" has a figurative meaning; it can and must be interpreted as the strength of will to fulfil his pledge to God.

Next, the Bible and history, so far as I remember, do not speak of prophets in the era of Judges, but relegate them to the era of Kings. I believe that Samson cannot be called prophet or prince or king of Israel.

Samson's hatred for the men of Judah is incomprehensible; in the time of Judges, Judea did not exist as a state; there was only a tribe of Judah living in southern Palestine, between the shores of the Dead Sea and the country of the Philistines.

The Danite tribe, Samson's tribe, lived somewhere in the valley of the Upper Jordan, on a line with the city of Sidon, far from the tribe of Judah. Why should Samson hate the tribe of Judah, which he probably did not know and with whom he had no relations? He might hate the people of his own tribe. There will be complaints about this, which you must prevent. Replace Judea with Israel throughout, where you must. This seems important to me.

Less important:

Samson's beard, dressed in *Assyrian fashion;* this is hardly probable or possible. The Philistines, a people of the Aryan branch, moved to Palestine from the shores of the Aegean Sea, it is assumed. They could scarcely have adopted the habits and customs of Assyria in the time of Judges.

There were no suits of armour at that time, only corselets are possible.

The existence of glass is doubtful.

It is hardly possible that the Jews had swords; they were a shepherd people and fought with slings and spears. Remember David's fight, which had taken place only a short time previously.

It is strange that Samson does not mention his tribe, the Danites, and also that he had a wife.

The first two acts are very well done, I think. The third drags, especially on pages five through eight. In the fourth, the drawn-out scene with the mother, and in the second scene, Samson's monologues are wearisome. And, by the way, Samson here resembles Vasilii Fiveiskii,[75] it seems to me.

144

Except for the first and third acts, Delilah is given too little importance, you forget her. And even in the third act she is carelessly presented.

Achimelek asks her twice:

"Is this true, Delilah?"

"You too, Delilah?"

She does not answer. And no stage directions.

She has remained obscure to me. What is there in her: just love? And this is not clear. She seems to need still another quality: repentance? Of course not. But fear of Dagon or a man because of her crime? Or an ambitious dream: if the prophet has been my lover and I have conquered him, why could not the prophet's God be my lover?

And why not contrast Delilah with the blind woman, the mother? This character does not seem to me sufficiently dramatic.

It would be better to make Pharaoh's love for Delilah more passionate.

Galian[76] chats in a refined way, but I do not think that the audience and the reader will understand his plans.

THE NOTES

NOTES TO LETTER 1

1 Before April 14, 1899; see *Daty zhizni i deiatel'nosti A. M. Gor'kogo* (*preimushchestvenno po materialam Departamenta Politsii*), in *Krasnyi arkhiv*, LXXVIII (1936), 23-84. (Abbreviated throughout as *Daty zhizni M. Gor'kogo*.)

2 One of the contributors to the Moscow newspaper *The Courier*, in which Leonid Andreev first began his literary activity. *The Courier* was published by L. A. Feigin [Fagin], starting November, 1897; I. D. Novik was secretary of the editorial board.

Probably the letter was written to Nikolai Petrovich Asheshov, who was well known in Samara and whom Gorky knew. Asheshov had been secretary of the editorial board of the *Samarskaia gazeta* (Samara Gazette) from 1894 to 1896. Gorky was living in Samara during this period and was a staff contributor to this paper; see A. Treplëv, "M. Gor'kii na Volge," in the volume *O Gor'kom sovremenniki* (Moscow, n.d.), p. 52. In 1899 Asheshov was working for *The Courier*.

NOTES TO LETTER 2

3 April 14, 1899; Gorky and Andreev were not yet personally acquainted.

4 V. S. Miroliubov, editor-publisher of the monthly *Zhurnal dlia vsekh* (Journal for All), published from 1898 to 1907; the journal was popular because it was cheap, yet the quality of its literary contributions was high. Gorky's attitude toward Miroliubov varied; he was ot in agreement with him from 1903 to 1911, then cooperated with him editorially on the journals *Zavety* (Legacy) and *Sovremennik* (The Contemporary) while both were abroad. Their voluminous correspondence has been published in the USSR; see *M. Gor'kii: materialy i issledovaniia*, III, 21-102.

NOTES TO LETTER 3

5 See Letter 2, note 4.

6 *Zhizn'*, a journal which was ideologically tinged with Legal Marxism. It was a trimonthly from January, 1897, to April, 1899, and a monthly from May, 1899, to April, 1901. The editors were M. S. Ermolaev and V. A. Posse.

7 *Mir Bozhii*, a monthly journal which was influenced by Legal Marxism; it appeared from 1892 to 1906. The editors were V. P. Ostrogorskii and A. Bogdanovich.

8 See Letter 2, note 4.

9 "Bargamot i Garas'ka," an early story by Leonid Andreev, published in the Moscow newspaper *The Courier* in 1898. Gorky praised this story in a letter to V. S. Miroliubov in 1898; see *M. Gor'kii: materialy i issledovaniia*, III, 24.

NOTES TO LETTER 4

10 Before Andreev sent Gorky his "Story about Sergei Petrovich."

11 See Letter 3, note 9.

12 "V Saburove," a story by Andreev published in *The Courier* on April 18, 1899.

13 V. A. Posse, organizer and one of the editors of the journal *Life*; see Letter 3, note 6.

NOTES TO LETTER 5

14 On the basis of police records; *Daty zhizni M. Gor'kogo*.

15 "Rasskaz o Sergee Petroviche," published October, 1900.

16 See Letter 3, note 6.

17 Pseudonym, Andreevich, 1866-1905, critic and historian of literature, member of the editorial board of *Life*.

18 See Letter 4, note 13.

NOTES TO LETTER 6

19 The newspaper *Birzhevye vedomosti* (Exchange Herald), a St. Petersburg publication. The paper had announced a literary competition.

20 See Letter 5, note 17.

21 Probably "The Story about Sergei Petrovich," see Letter 5, note 15.

22 See Letter 3, note 9. Gorky calls the story "The Hippopotamus (*begemot*) and the Batman."

23 See Letter 4, note 12.

NOTE TO LETTER 7

24 See Letter 4, note 13.

NOTES TO LETTER 8

25 See Letter 4, note 13.

26 See Letter 5, note 15.

NOTES TO LETTER 9

27 The "conflict with the public" took place in the autumn of 1900 in the Moscow Art Theater, on the premises of the former Hermitage Theater. During the intermission a group of spectators started to rap on the door of the director's box, where Gorky was sitting, and to call for him to come out to them. Gorky went out and sharply reprimanded the spectators for intruding and for being tactlessly curious. The papers, exaggerating this unimportant incident, distorted the facts; they attributed coarse language to Gorky and expanded the story. The conservative newspapers took advantage of the chance to square accounts with the leftist writer. The writer N. D. Teleshov, a witness of the incident, established the truth and defended Gorky in a letter to the editor of *The Courier*, which was printed in issue No. 319, November 17, 1900; see N. D. Teleshov, *Zapiski pisatelia* (Moscow, 1950), p. 94. Andreev responded in an article printed in *The Courier*, "Russkii chelovek i znamenitost'," 1900; the article is reprinted in *Sobrannye sochineniia* (Collected Works), A. F. Marks edition, published in St. Petersburg as a premium to the magazine *Niva*, 1913, VI, 231-33.

28 Pseudonym for Vladimir Aleksandrovich Ashkinazi, theatrical correspondent for the newspapers *Novosti dnia* and *Sankt-Peterburgskie vedomosti*; an untrue report appeared in the latter.

29 See Letter 3, note 6.

NOTES TO LETTER 10

30 Organized in Nizhnii Novgorod.

31 Gorky's reference here is unclear. The reference may be to the story which Andreev' later wrote about prostitution, "Khristiane" (The Christians), 1905.

32 Stepan Gavrilovich Petrov, 1868-1941, a poet with a rebellious nature who used to make successful appearances at concerts, where he read his own verses and stories, accompanying himself on a *gusli*, a Russian instrument resembling a psaltery. The pseudonym "Skitalets" (vagabond) was invented by Gorky. Gorky's nickname for him was "Gavrilych."

33 T. I. Polner, 1864-1935, a journalist who used to write a great deal about the socially useful role of the zemstvo institutions.

NOTES TO LETTER 11

34 Viktor Aleksandrovich Gol'tsev, 1850-1906, member of the editorial board of the journal *Russkaia mysl'* (Russian Thought), whom Gorky disliked because of his moderate liberalism.

35 Possibly Gorky refers to the woman who was to be Andreev's first wife, Alexandra Mikhailovna Veligorskaia.

36 See Letter 1, note 2.

NOTES TO LETTER 12

37 It is impossible to ascertain what publication Gorky refers to.

38 Probably a reference to the incident in the theater; see Letter 9, note 27. The intimate nature of this letter, however, greatly obscures the contents.

39 See Letter 10, note 32.

NOTES TO LETTER 13

40 See Letter 10.

41 Abram Evgenievich Kaufman, writer (see his "Vospominaniia o L. Andreeve" in *Vestnik literatury*, 1920, No. 9).

42 Arkadii Pavlovich Alekseevskii, later editor of the newspaper *Utro Rossii* (Morning of Russia).

43 Gorky's own version of an untranslatable Russian saying.

44 E. N. Chirikov, 1864-1932, writer.

45 See Letter 10, note 32.

46 Gorky introduced Christmas trees for the poor children of the streets (see A. Treplëv, "M. Gor'kii na Volge," in *O Gor'kom sovremenniki*, [Moscow: T-vo pisatelei, 1928], p. 77). In 1900 a group of Gorky's friends and admirers, with the financial support of a Nizhnii Novgorod benefactor, the Old Believer Bugrov, arranged such a Christmas tree and provided presents for four or five thousand children (see A. Svobodov, "Iz rannikh zametok Gor'kogo," *Pechat' i revoliutsiia*, 1927, No. 1, pp. 19-28, in which Gorky's appeal for contributions, "Nechto o Elke," *Nizhegorodskii listok*, 1900, No. 9, is mentioned).

47 These are Russian proverbs, with variations, for which exact English equivalents could not be found.

NOTES TO LETTER 14

48 See Letter 1, note 2.

49 The Sunday of the week following Easter week, called in Russian "Fomina" week. In 1901, Fomina week fell between April 8 and 14.

50 "Zhili-byli," a story by Andreev written between February 5 and 16, 1901.

NOTES TO LETTER 15

51 Probably a reference to payment for "The Story about Sergei Petrovich," published in *Life*, October, 1900; see Letter 5, note 15.

52 See Letter 3, note 6.

53 See Letter 1, note 2.

54 Writer, 1863-1922, with whom Gorky was acquainted; he spent a vacation with him in the country from June 10 to 24, 1899.

NOTE TO LETTER 16

55 See Letter 15, note 51.

NOTES TO LETTER 17

56 According to police records, Gorky was in St. Petersburg from February 22 to March 8 (*Daty zhizni M. Gor'kogo*).

57 Easter week in 1901 fell between April 1 and 7.

58 Correctly Filippov, an insignificant poet.

59 "Burevestnik," a revolutionary poem by Gorky published in *Life* in April, 1901, which led the censor to forbid the publication of this journal. The police administration in late 1900 and early 1901 watched Gorky closely on his frequent trips to Moscow and St. Petersburg. On April 16, 1901, during the night, Gorky's house in Nizhnii Novgorod was searched, and he was arrested and jailed.

60 See Letter 11, note 34.

61 Possibly a reference to the student demonstration in St. Petersburg on March 4, 1901, in protest against the new student regulations which resulted in 183 students of Kiev University being conscripted into the army. Gorky apparently witnessed the dispersal of the student meeting at Kazan Cathedral in St. Petersburg.

62 A progressive cooperative publishing house, the chief organizer of which was K. P. Piatnitskii, with Gorky assisting. The publishing house lasted from 1898 to 1913; before 1904 individual works by Russian and foreign writers were published. After 1904, volumes of creative literature by the *Znanie* Cooperative were issued; by 1913 about forty such volumes had appeared.

63 "V temnuiu dal'," an early story by Andreev, written in 1900. Gorky valued this story highly.

64 Henri Lichtenberger, an author of books on Nietzsche's philosophy and on socialism and the French Revolution.

65 O. N. Popova, a woman publisher.

NOTE TO LETTER 18 (Telegram)

66 This signature may have been a political camouflage.

NOTES TO LETTER 19

67 Could not be identified.

68 Gorky's second play was *Na dne* (The Lower Depths), written in July, 1902, in Arzamas.

69 Nestor Vasil'evich Kukol'nik, 1809-1868, a popular Russian dramatist of the first half of the nineteenth century, the author of bombastic plays which were completely out of fashion and forgotten in the last half of the century; the contrast with Shakespeare is ironic.

70 See Letter 1, note 2.

71 *Nizhegorodskii listok*, Nizhnii Novgorod newspaper.

72 *Severnyi krai*, newspaper of the Volga area.

73 *Volzhskii vestnik*, newspaper of the Volga area.

74 *Samarskaia gazeta*, Samara newspaper; see Letter 1, note 2.

NOTES TO LETTER 20

75 The phrases "I am living in my old apartment," "write my wife," and "your letter reached me" permits us to suppose that Gorky was either in a Nizhnii Novgorod jail or under house arrest; see Letters 17 and 21.

76 Just what story of Andreev's Gorky has in mind here is unclear.

77 *Russkoe bogatstvo*, a serious and influential monthly, published from 1876 to 1918. The influential Narodnik critic N. K. Mikhailovskii was on its board of editors.

78 Gorky assumed, after *Life* was forced to cease publication (see Letter 17, note 59), that he would succeed in organizing a similar journal under another title; later Posse organized the Legal Marxist journal *Novoe slovo* (New Word).

79 The journal *Pravda* (Truth), a monthly for art, literature, and discussion of public questions, was published in Moscow from January, 1904 to 1906. The idea of a journal called *Pravda* as a Bolshevist organ was developed much later.

80 Journalist, translator, and publisher.

81 Fëdor Ivanovich Shaliapin, 1873-1938, famous Russian concert and opera singer.

NOTES TO LETTER 21

82 Andreev's first volume of stories, published by the *Znanie* publishers in 1901. This book contained the stories mentioned in this letter.

83 See Letter 5.

84 See Letter 20, note 80.

85 Possibly Gorky is referring to the first draft of his play *The Lower Depths*, which he finished during the summer of 1902.

86 Byzantine scholar and historian.

87 From April 17 to May 17, 1901, Gorky was in jail in Nizhnii Novgorod. On May 17 he was subjected to house arrest. On June 3

he was released and subjected to special police supervision. On September 17, 1901, Gorky was ordered by the government to be sent away from Nizhnii Novgorod to the little town of Arzamas, in the Nizhnii Novgorod province. The town had an extremely unhealthy climate which would have been fatal for Gorky, who had a tendency toward tuberculosis of the lungs. Gorky, with the support of his physicians, demanded permission to go to the Crimea for a rest cure, and on October 16 this was permitted, provided he did not stay in Yalta. After his stay in the Crimea, however, Gorky was obliged to live from May to August, 1902, in exile in Arzamas.

NOTES TO LETTER 22

88 Written after Gorky had been informed of the decision to send him to Arzamas (September 17, 1901) and before he left for the Crimea (November 7). Gorky received permission for the trip on October 16.

89 Vasilii Vasilievich Brusianin, 1867-1919, author.

90 See Letter 20, note 77.

91 See Letter 21, note 87.

NOTES TO LETTER 23

92 See Letter 19, note 71; Gorky was a staff contributor to this newspaper from 1899 to 1905.

93 Aleksei Vasil'evich Iarovitskii, a regular contributor to the paper, never developed into an important writer. His pseudonym was "Kornev."

NOTES TO LETTER 24

94 Theatrical producer, writer, and with Stanislavskii founder in 1898 of the Moscow Art Theater.

95 Could not be identified. Possibly a distortion of Sablin (see Letter 20, note 80).

96 "Stena," a story by Andreev, finished September 4, 1901.

97 Apparently the Moscow Art Theater agreed to present *Meshchane* (The Petty Bourgeois), translated into English as *The Smug Citizen*, in *Poet Lore* (Boston), XVII (1906), No. 4, 1-74, Gorky's first play, written in 1901. On the presentation of this play, its dress rehearsal, and first performance, which took place in St. Petersburg, not in

Moscow, when the theater was on tour in late March, 1902, see the letter from the singer Sobinov, published in M. L'vov, *Sobinov* (Moscow, 1951), p. 25. On the first presentations of Gorky's plays at the Moscow Art Theater, see the article by V. Luzhskii, the oldest actor in the theater, in *Pechat' i revoliutsiia*, 1928, No. 4, pp. 28-32.

NOTES TO LETTER 25

98 Correctly, Lëv Abramovich Fagin; see Letter 1, note 2.

99 See Letter 19, note 71, and Letter 23, note 92.

1 Perhaps Gorky means his play *The Petty Bourgeois*; see Letter 24, note 97.

2 See Letter 20, note 80.

3 On November 7, 1901, according to the police records, Gorky left for the Crimea, via Moscow and Khar'kov; see Letter 27.

NOTE TO LETTER 26

4 The youth of Nizhnii Novgorod, who adored Gorky, arranged a mass send-off and demonstration for the disgraced writer and scattered hectographed leaflets containing revolutionary material at the station. They also informed people at the main points along the route taken by Gorky and his family so that they could honour him and make a protest against the government. The demonstrations were broken up by the police and the young people were dispersed (see Letter 27, note 5). Gorky apparently is referring to an incident which took place in Khar'kov on November 9, 1901, when the police resorted to physical force (see N. D. Teleshov, *Zapiski pisatelia* [Moscow, 1950], 99-102). Probably the young people wanted to present to Gorky works by Tolstoy or a portrait of him.

NOTE TO LETTER 27

5 This and the previous letter reveal the growing intimacy between Gorky and Andreev; the former polite form, *vy*, has been replaced by the intimate *ty*, and this practice is followed in subsequent letters. The transfer to *ty*, according to N. D. Teleshov, in *Zapiski pisatelia* (Moscow, 1950), pages 122-30, occurred on November 8, 1901, when Gorky was passing through Moscow to the Crimea (see Letter 26).

The policemaster of Moscow arranged for Gorky's car to be put on a siding outside Moscow, in Podol'sk, to wait for the Moscow train for the Crimea. When Gorky's friends learned of this, they hurried to Podol'sk to meet Gorky. At that time Gorky declared that from then on he would call all those who had come to meet him *ty*. Andreev was among these friends.

NOTES TO LETTER 28

6 A nickname for Skitalets (see Letter 10, note 32).

7 This is not clear; possibly the writers were preparing a letter of congratulation for the famous singer, at that time a friend of Gorky's, Fëdor Ivanovich Shaliapin who may have appeared at a benefit performance; see Letter 20, note 81.

8 Piatnitskii; see Letter 17, note 62.

9 Probably a payment to Andreev from the *Znanie* publishing house. Volume I of Andreev's work was first published by *Znanie* in 1901, was quickly sold out, and was reprinted. By 1906 the first volume had already reached the ninth edition. The volume was expanded by the inclusion of new stories; Gorky participated in the selection of stories.

NOTES TO LETTER 29

10 Piatnitskii; see Letter 17, note 62.

11 Ivan Alekseevich Bunin, 1870-1954, at that time a beginning writer, subsequently a celebrated Russian writer and the only one to receive the Nobel Prize.

12 "A. S. Serafimovich" (pseudonym for A. S. Popov), 1863-1949, a writer who joined the Communist Party after the Revolution.

13 See Letter 28.

NOTES TO LETTER 30

14 The sequence of Letters 30 through 36 could not be established.

15 See Letter 17, note 62.

16 "Nabat," November, 1901.

17 "Smekh," January, 1901.

18 "V podvale," an early story.

19 The letter is apparently concerned with the contents of a new

edition of the first volume of the Andreev stories; it had been favorably criticized, particularly by N. R. Mikhailovskii in the November *Russian Riches*, 1901 (see Letter 20, note 77).

20 "Bezdna," finished January 10, 1902. This story incurred sharp criticism in the Press for immorality. Tolstoy's wife, Sof'ia Andreevna, in particular protested in *New Times*; and *Russian Herald*, *News of the Day*, and *The Courier* all asked their readers' opinion of this story (see Fatov, *Molodye gody L. Andreeva* [Moscow, 1924], p. 185.)

21 "Pet'ka na dache," September, 1899.

22 Perhaps "Inostranets" (The Foreigner), written in 1902, is meant here.

23 "Mysl'," April, 1902, first published in *God's World*. When this letter was written the story was not yet finished, but Gorky knew of the plan for it.

24 "Bunt na korable"; no story by this name was later published. Perhaps this plan was completed much later in the play *Okean* (Ocean).

25 Andreev's marriage to Alexandra Mikhailovna Veligorskaia took place on February 10, 1902.

NOTES TO LETTER 31

26 See Letter 23, note 93.

27 The volume was dedicated to Gorky.

28 See Letter 30, note 18.

29 Concerning preparations for a new edition of Andreev's works (see Letter 30, note 19).

30 "Kusaka," a story by Andreev published in 1901.

31 "Sluchai," a story by Andreev published in 1901.

32 E. Ganeizer, editor of *Peterburgskie vedomosti* (Petersburg Herald); his article, "The Bewitched Streetlamp," on Gorky and Chekhov, appeared in the December 25, 1901, issue.

33 Pseudonym for Iuliia Ivanovna Iakovleva, a minor authoress.

34 A pseudonym used by Andreev to sign articles in *The Courier*.

35 See Letter 1, note 2.

36 See Letter 23, note 93.

NOTES TO LETTER 32

37 Apparently refers to Letter 33. Published in *M. Gor'kii: materialy i issledovaniia*, I, 140.

38 See Letter 30, note 23.

39 See Letter 2, note 4.

40 See Letter 20, note 77.

41 See Letter 3, note 7.

42 Vladimir Galaktionovich Korolenko, 1853-1921, prominent writer and progressive public figure. He attended the Petrovsk Academy of Agriculture and Forestry but had been forced to leave for political reasons.

43 See Letter 3, note 7.

44 Published as "Vasilii Fiveiskii" (The Life of Vasilii Fiveiskii); finished November 19, 1903, published in 1904 in the *Znanie Literary Volume No. 1*.

NOTES TO LETTER 33

45 This letter may be in response to Letter 32, from Andreev to Gorky; see Letter 32, and Letter 30, note 23.

46 See Letter 17, note 63.

47 Vladimir Andreevich Gringmut, editor of the conservative newspaper *Moskovskie vedomosti* (Moscow Herald).

48 Vladimir Petrovich Meshcherskii, 1839-1914, extreme right-wing publicist and writer, editor of the newspaper *Grazhdanin* (Citizen).

49 Mikhail Osipovich Men'shikov, 1859-1918, a biting, influential conservative contributor to the St. Petersburg newspaper *Novoe vremia* (New Times). The liberals called him "Judas." He was executed by Soviet punitive forces.

50 V. Rozanov, 1859-1919, a contributor to the newspaper *New Times* and author of books that expressed rightist political views.

51 Dmitrii Sergeevich Merezhkovskii, 1865-1941, outstanding critic and writer.

52 N. D. Teleshov, realistic writer. His *Zapiski pisatelia* (Notes of a Writer) (Moscow, 1950) forms an important source of information on Gorky's activities (see, for example, Letter 9, note 27; Letter 26, note 4; and Letter 27, note 5).

53 See Letter 13, note 44.

54 See Letter 17, note 62.

55 See Letter 30, note 16.

56 See Letter 24, note 96.

57 See Letter 32 and Letter 30, note 23.

58 See Letter 20, note 77. Mikhailovskii reviewed Andreev's first book favorably in *Russian Riches*, Issue 11. He subsequently refused "Thought," which Andreev sent to him on Gorky's recommendation; it was published in *God's World* (1902), No. 7 (see Letter 3, note 7).

59 Possibly a reference to Count M. N. Murav'ëv, who persecuted the Polish nationalists in the 1860s and was notorious for his repressive administration.

60 See Letter 13, note 44.

61 "Lëv Issakovich Shestov" (pseudonym for Shvartsman), 1866-1938, a literary philosopher whose views approached those of Merezhkovskii's circle.

62 Pseudonym for the critic and publicist Mikhail Petrovich Miklashevskii, a Menshevist, who wrote the preface to the Russian edition of Lichtenbergers *Philosophy of Nietzsche*.

63 See Letter 17, note 64.

64 Vasilii Iakovlevich Bogucharskii, 1861-1915, historian of the revolutionary movement in Russia, a politican cooperating with the Socialist Revolutionaries.

65 See Letter 29, note 12.

66 See Letter 3, note 6, and Letter 4, note 13.

67 See Letter 1, note 2.

68 Could not be identified.

NOTES TO LETTER 34

69 Possibly *Journal for All* (see Letter 2, note 4).

70 "Troe," a story by Gorky, written in 1900, published in *Zhizn'*, 1900, Nos. 11-12, and 1901, Nos. 1-4.

71 See Letter 30, note 25.

72 See Letter 1, note 2.

73 "Ivan Pavlovich Miroliubov," pseudonym for Iuvachev, author of reminiscences of Sakhalin and Schlusselburg Prison.

74 Viktor Sergeevich Miroliubov; see Letter 2, note 4.

NOTES TO LETTER 35

75 See Letter 30, note 19.

76 See Letter 17, note 62.

77 A minor critic who wrote about Andreev; Gorky's reference here is ironic.

78 This story could not be identified.
79 See Letter 34, note 73.

NOTES TO LETTER 36

80 See Letter 30, note 25.
81 Alexander Aleksin, Gorky's physician and friend.

NOTES TO LETTER 37

82 Andreev's story "Thought," finished April, 1902. In the final version, Andreev finished the story with the word "nothing," as Gorky advised.
83 See Letter 10, note 32.
84 The *Znanie* edition of Andreev's stories.

NOTE TO LETTER 38

85 The letter heading of this notepaper does not designate the date or the place from which it was written. Gorky probably had the letterhead because he was a member of *Znanie*.

NOTES TO LETTER 39

86 Piatnitskii; see Letter 17, note 62.
87 See Letter 37. The editor of *Russian Riches*, N. K. Mikhailovskii, refused to publish "Thought" because the subject matter and the concept of the hero were psychopathological. It was published in *God's World*.
88 See Letter 10, note 32.

NOTES TO LETTER 40

89 S. A. Skirmunt, 1863-1932, publisher. Police records show that Gorky stayed in Skirmunt's apartment (*Daty zhizni M. Gor'kogo*).
90 Piatnitskii; see Letter 17, note 62.

NOTES TO LETTER 41 (Telegram)

91 The notation on the telegram is not clear.
92 This reference could not be identified.

NOTES TO LETTER 42

93 Apparently a reference to some unpleasant incident in which Andreev, who suffered from chronic alcoholism, became drunk and offended several people.

94 See Letter 36, note 81.

95 Unidentified acquaintance of both writers.

96 Unidentified acquaintance of both writers.

97 Evgenii Andreevich Andreevich-Solov'ëv, a critic from the journal *Life* (see Letter 5, note 17).

NOTES TO LETTER 43

98 Refers to Andreev's story, "Original'nyi chelovek" (Original Fellow), finished October 24, 1902.

99 No such "document" could be found with the letter.

1 Like "Lady Shura," a humorous term of affection for Andreev's wife.

NOTES TO LETTER 44

2 "Noch'." Author unknown.

3 See Letter 30, note 20.

4 See Letter 10, note 32.

5 "The Tenor," apparently a story which Andreev had considered writing but never finished and never published.

6 See Letter 17, note 62.

NOTES TO LETTER 45

7 See Letter 44, note 5.

8 See Letter 10, note 32.

9 Unidentified.

10 See Letter 39.

11 A minor writer.

NOTES TO LETTER 46

12 The birth of Andreev's first child was due. The eldest son was Vadim Andreev (see his reminiscences of his father, "Povest' ob ottse,"

in the *émigré* monthly *Russkie zapiski* [Paris, May-December, 1938]).
Gorky was expecting to be the child's godfather.

13 See Letter 40, note 89.

14 A minor writer.

NOTES TO LETTER 47

15 *Kum*, or father of Gorky's godchild, denoting a close personal relation between two men. Gorky is apparently suggesting here that he could be literally the godfather of his friend's child (see Letter 46).

16 See Letter 10, note 32.

17 See Letter 1, note 2.

18 Savva Abramovich Sorin, b. 1878.

19 See Letter 13, note 42. What incident Gorky is referring to could not be discovered.

20 Valerii Iakovlevich Briusov, 1873-1924, symbolist poet who later turned to "social themes" and joined the Communist Party after the Revolution.

21 Vasilii M. Doroshevich, 1864-1920, well-known publicist and contributor to the liberal Moscow newspaper *Russkoe slovo* (Russian Word).

22 See Letter 1, note 2.

23 Alexander Nikolaevich Benois, a distinguished Russian artist and scholar of art history, at that time a spokesman for the "decadent" society *Mir iskusstva* (World of Art).

24 See Letter 30, note 24.

25 Pavel Ivanovich Novgorodtsev, 1866-1924, a professor of philosophy and a Kantian idealist.

26 See Letter 30, note 22.

27 See Letter 46, note 12.

NOTES TO LETTER 48

28 The sixteenth-century church in Red Square in Moscow.

29 The most important Moscow art museum.

30 Now the Lenin Library, the largest library in Moscow, which also has a large collection of works of art.

31 Probably a benefit performance for Fëdor Shaliapin (see Letter 20, note 81).

32 See Letter 17, note 62.

33 Instead of *lozha*, Gorky uses *rozha* ("kisser"; "mug").

NOTES TO LETTER 49

34 See Letter 40, note 89.

35 Gorky proposed to include in the volume Russian writers and public figures who were born or lived in Nizhnii Novgorod. They would "participate" to the extent that excerpts from their writings or articles commemorating them would appear.

36 Minin and Pozharskii, national heroes, who led a popular insurrection in 1611 against the Polish seizure of Russian territory and helped to crown Mikhail Fëdorovich Romanov, the first Romanov, tsar. Both were born in Nizhnii Novgorod.

37 Patriarch Nikon, 1605-1681, reformer of the Orthodox Church, son of a peasant of the Nizhnii Novgorod region.

38 Old Believer priest, 1620-1681, who led the protests against Nikon's reforms. Born in Nizhnii Novgorod.

39 N. A. Dobroliubov, 1836-1861, well-known literary critic, from Nizhnii Novgorod.

40 I. P. Kulibin, 1735-1818, a widely known self-taught engineer, son of a Nizhnii Novgorod tradesman.

41 M. M. Speranskii, 1772-1839, famous government official under Alexander I, who was exiled to Nizhnii Novgorod because of reforms he had proposed.

42 A. S. Pushkin, 1799-1837, great Russian poet, who had referred to Nizhnii Novgorod in his writings.

43 Pëtr Dmitrievich Boborykin, 1836-1921, popular writer of the time.

44 See Letter 32, note 42.

45 Sergei Iakovlevich Elpat'evskii, 1854-1933, progressive writer, public leader, and physician.

46 Probably Innokentii Fëdorovich Annenskii, 1856-1909, poet and translator.

47 See Letter 13, note 44.

48 Shatalets, "Staggerer," a humorous nickname for Skitalets (see Letter 10, note 32).

49 A *Literary Volume No.* 1 of *Znanie* was published in 1904. The

Nizhnii Novgorod volume came out only in 1905 and its contents bore little resemblance to the initial plan. The volume contained short stories, sketches, and articles. Andreev contributed "Mel'kom," (For a Moment), "Ben-Tobit," and "Marseillaise."

50 See Letter 30, note 24.

NOTES TO LETTER 50

51 Miroliubov; see Letter 2, note 4. After Miroliubov used a picture of Gorky and his son as a frontispiece without Gorky's permission in *Journal for All*, 1903, No. 2, Gorky broke off relations with him until 1911; Gorky was also annoyed by Miroliubov's inconsistency in permitting the modernists, symbolists, and "pornographers," particularly Artsybashev, to publish in his journal.

52 Intentional misspellings.

53 *Novyi put'*, a modernist journal, published from 1903 to 1904, which Gorky considered abstract, divorced from practical life, and hostile to the progressive movement.

54 Possibly *Truth*; see Letter 20, note 79.

NOTES TO LETTER 51

55 Reference not clear. *Truth* published Andreev's story "Gubernator" (The Governor) in 1905 and incurred repressive censorship because of it. It is improbable that Gorky could have known of this story so far in advance.

56 See Letter 36, note 81.

57 See Letter 20, note 79.

58 See Letter 10, note 32.

NOTES TO LETTER 53

59 See Letter 2, note 4. Miroliubov apparently turned down one of Andreev's stories (probably "Red Laugh," which was very antimilitaristic). See also Letter 50, note 51.

60 Apparently a satirical name; the reference could not be identified.

61 This story was never published. Andreev incorporated some of its elements into his play *Tsar Golod* (King Hunger), 1907. Some other aspects apparently were included in the story "Tak bylo" (So It Was).

62 See Letter 50, note 53.

63 These are doggerel verses which Gorky apparently invented on the spur of the moment as he was writing the letter. The translator has endeavored to convey the meaning, meter, rhyme scheme, and general flavor of the original; no effort has been made to "improve" on the original by smoothing out the translation.

64 A satirical distortion of the name Vladimir Osipovich Trachtenberg, a second-rate writer and the author of the trilogy *Yesterday*, *Today*, and *Tomorrow*.

65 Andreev's wife.

66 Alexander Ivanovich Kosorotov, a journalist with the pseudonym "Shmel'," a contributor to the newspaper *Russia* in 1903 and 1904.

NOTES TO LETTER 54

67 See Letter 49, note 35.

68 Nikolai Ivanovich Iordanskii, 1876-1928, journalist and Menshevik publicist. After 1905 he became a member of the editorial board of *Sovremennyi mir* (Contemporary World).

69 See Letter 17, note 62.

70 *Znanie Literary Volumes No.* 1 and *No.* 2, for 1903 were published in St. Petersburg in 1904.

71 Gorky's third play was *Dachniki*, translated into English in *Poet Lore* (Boston), XVI (1905), No. 3, 1-90, as *The Summer Folk*.

72 *Vesy*, an organ of the modernists and symbolists; the poet Briusov took an active part in it. Gorky was hostile to the journal.

73 Written after the outbreak of the Russo-Japanese War.

NOTES TO LETTER 55

74 Chekhov's funeral took place in Moscow on July 9, 1904.

75 See Letter 17, note 62.

76 Alexander Ivanovich Kuprin, 1870-1938, well-known writer.

77 See Letter 29, note 11.

78 See Letter 30, note 24, and Letter 53, note 61.

79 Andreev's wife.

NOTES TO LETTER 56

80 A reference to the Russo-Japanese War, January 26, 1904, to August 23, 1905. Gorky was hostile to the patriotic attitude expressed in most of the press.

81 N. A. Engelhardt, critic and contributor to the conservative St. Petersburg newspaper *Novoe vremia* (New Times).

82 See Letter 43, note 98.

83 "Vikentii Vikent'evich Veresaev," pseudonym for Smidovich, 1867-1945, writer and physician.

84 Andreev's wife.

85 The name of the town could not be discovered.

NOTES TO LETTER 57

86 The original is a humorous fantasy with many plays on words. On page 16 there is a photograph of part of the original manuscript. Almost the entire letter is written in metrical prose, in trochaic tetrameter.

87 Henry Neville Hutchinson, author of a popular book on paleontology, *Extinct Monsters* (New York: Appleton, 1892), published in translation as *Vymershie chudovishcha* by Znanie, 1903-1904.

88 On February 21, 1902, Gorky, as well as V. G. Korolenko and A. P. Chekhov, was elected by a joint session of the Division of Russian Language and Literature of the Imperial Academy of Sciences an honorary academician in fine arts. On March 10, 1902, however, at the tsar's request, the elections were declared void because Gorky was under investigation for his political activities. Out of loyalty to him, Chekhov and Korolenko renounced the title of academician. See A. Derman, "Akademicheskii intsident," in *O Gor'kom sovremenniki* (Moscow: T-vo pisatelei, 1928), 205-55.

89 See Letter 17, note 62.

90 See Letter 54, note 72.

91 See Letter 56, note 80.

92 Apparently material for the volume to be published in honor of Chekhov (see Letter 55).

93 Miroliubov; see Letter 2, note 4.

NOTES TO LETTER 58

94 *Nasha zhizn'*, a leftist newspaper, published from November 6, 1904, to December 31, 1905.

95 See Letter 31, note 34.

96 Chirikov; see Letter 13, note 44.

97 Nickname for Skitalets; see Letter 10, note 32.

NOTES TO LETTER 59

98 According to police records, Gorky was active in St. Petersburg and Moscow at this time (*Daty zhizni M. Gor'kogo*).

99 Gorky was expecting Andreev to send him the manuscript for "Krasnyi smekh" (Red Laugh).

1 See Letter 29, note 11.

2 See Letter 55, note 76.

3 See Letter 54, note 71.

4 Skitalets; see Letter 10, note 32, and Letter 49, note 48.

5 The Moscow Art Theater only gave a reading of Gorky's play; see V. Luzhskii's reminiscences in *Pechat' i revoliutsiia*, 1928, No. 4, 28-32. The play was first produced in Nezlobin's private theater in Riga in 1904, and possibly this company came to St. Petersburg on tour that year.

6 Merezhkovskii (see Letter 33, note 51), Dmitrii Vladimirovich Filosofov, b. 1872, and S. P. Diaghilev, 1872-1929 (subsequently famous abroad as a promoter of Russian ballet, opera, and music) were all participants in *New Path* (see Letter 50, note 53) and *Mir iskusstva* (World of Art), 1898-1904 (see Letter 47, note 23).

7 *Peterburgskie vedomosti* (Petersburg Herald)(see Letter 31, note 32), *Svet* (World), and *Peterburgskaia gazeta* (Petersburg Gazette) were hostile to Gorky.

8 See Letter 53, note 66.

9 See Letter 58, note 94.

10 Pseudonym for Miklashevskii. See Letter 33, note 62.

11 Mar'ia Fëdorovna Andreeva, b. 1872, an actress, at first appeared at the Moscow Art Theatre, where she became acquainted with Gorky, and later took part in Nezlobin's private theater in Riga until she went abroad with Gorky (see Letter 77, note 21). In 1904 she broke off her marriage with her husband, Zheliabuzhskii, a high official, joined the Bolsheviks, and became Gorky's mistress. In 1912 she returned to Russia illegally and again joined Nezlobin's private theater. After 1917 she took an active part in public life and was commissar of the Leningrad theaters. From 1931 to 1948 she was director of the Moscow House of Scholars.

12 Ignatii Nikolaevich Potapenko, 1856-1929, a writer popular at the time.

13 Mar'ia Fëdorovna Andreeva.

14 See Letter 17, note 62.

15 See note 10, this letter, and Letter 33, note 62.

NOTE TO LETTER 60

16 Andreev's story "Krasnyi smekh" (Red Laugh), finished November 8, 1904. Gorky is describing his impressions of the story in this letter. It was first published in the third *Znanie* Volume in 1905 after the editor of *Journal for All*, Miroliubov, rejected it because it was unpatriotic. The story is composed of fictional excerpts from a journal. Andreev apparently followed Gorky's advice on only one or two minor points before publishing it.

NOTES TO LETTER 61

17 Reference unclear; possibly "Krasnyi smekh" (Red Laugh) (see Letter 60).

18 The writers of the *Znanie* Cooperative frequently sent their stories for publication to Berlin in case the censor forbade their publication in Russia.

19 See Letter 29, note 11.

20 Serafimovich; see Letter 29, note 12.

21 This may refer to the anthology being published in honor of Chekhov (see Letter 55). The *Znanie Literary Volume No. 3*, was published in 1905 and contained Andreev's "Red Laugh."

NOTES TO LETTER 62

22 See Letter 55.

23 See Letter 55, note 76.

24 See Letter 54, note 71, and Letter 59, note 5.

25 Pseudonym for Sergei Aleksandrovich Alekseev, 1869–1922, a dramatist who became famous for his *Deti Vaniushina* (Children of Vaniushin). Gorky refers to his play *Avdot'ina zhizn'* (Avdotia's Life), 1904–1905.

26 Skitalets; see Letter 10, note 32.

27 See Letter 29, note 11.

28 Piatnitskii; see Letter 17, note 62.

29 See Letter 13, note 44.

30 Sergei Ivanovich Gusev-Orenburgskii, b. 1867, writer, first published in the *Znanie Literary Volume No. 4*. Now living in the United States.

31 Stories by Andreev. "The Little Negro" was actually called "An Original Fellow" (see Letter 43, note 98).

32 See Letter 49.

33 Gorky was going to Riga to evade government repressions. According to police records, Gorky was arrested on January 10, 1905, for his participation in revolutionary activities on January 4 to 9. He escaped to Riga, but on January 11 he was again arrested and sent to St. Petersburg, where he was imprisoned in the Trubetskoi Bastion of the Fortress of Peter and Paul. On January 15 he was brought to the gendarme section for questioning, and on February 12 he was assigned to the House of Preliminary Imprisonment because of ill-health. On February 14 he was released on 10,000 ruble bail on condition that he remain in Riga. He left for Riga that very day (*Daty zhizni M. Gor'kogo*, also V. V. Rudnev, *Gor'kii-revoliutsioner*, pp. 67–68).

NOTES TO LETTER 63

34 Andreeva; see Letter 59, note 11.

35 Grand Prince Sergei Aleksandrovich, fourth son of Emperor Alexander II, b. 1857, assassinated by a bomb thrown by the SR Kaliaev, February 4, 1905. The Grand Prince was Governor General of Moscow from February 26, 1891, and severely prosecuted "leftist elements."

36 Dmitrii Fëdorovich Trepov, 1855–1906, until January 11, 1905, Chief of Police in Moscow. He was then appointed Governor General of St. Petersburg. He was hated as a severe reactionary.

37 Andreev had apparently informed Gorky of the police measures introduced in Moscow.

38 A. N. Kuropatkin, General of Infantry, unsuccessful Chief of Staff during the Russo-Japanese War.

39 Gorky opposed Tolstoy's doctrine of "non-resistance to evil."

40 Skitalets; see Letter 10, note 32.

NOTES TO LETTER 64 (Telegram)

41 Reference uncertain. Possibly the telegram refers to Andreev's story "Prizraki" (Phantoms), finished October 11, 1904.

42 Andreeva; see Letter 59, note 11.

NOTES TO LETTER 65

43 Refers to a draft of an appeal by the Moscow writers to the government, following the outbreak of revolutionary activities, urging government reform. Gorky opposed the appeal as he had already adopted a completely revolutionary viewpoint.

44 Pacific port captured by the Japanese, surrendered by General Stessel' on December 20, 1904. The press urged that Stössel be treated leniently.

45 See Letter 60, note 16.

46 See Letter 53, note 61.

47 Andreev's wife.

48 See Letter 11, note 34.

49 M. P. Artsybashev, 1878-1927, a writer whose works contained pornographic elements. Gorky is referring to his story "Smert' Lande" (Death of Landé), which was published at the end of 1904 in Miroliubov's *Journal for All* (see Letter 2, note 4).

NOTES TO LETTER 66

50 According to police records, Gorky left for Yalta without permission (see Letter 62, note 33).

51 See Letter 10, note 32.

52 Savva Timofeevich Morozov, 1862-1905, a rich merchant who used to furnish Gorky with funds for the revolutionary movement.

53 See Letter 1, note 2.

54 See Letter 13, note 44.

55 See Letter 59, note 11.

56 P. Orlenev, an actor who portrayed Oswald in Ibsen's *Ghosts*.

NOTES TO LETTER 67

57 The police records state that Gorky lived in the country in Finland after his return from Yalta. On August 6 he left for Moscow, on August 16 he returned to Finland, on September 1 he went to St. Petersburg, and on September 12 he arrived in Moscow. The phrase "send an answer by the cabman" suggests that the letter was written from Moscow, where Andreev lived.

58 Station on the Finnish railroad.

59 Probably this was one of the devices used by the liberal intellectuals to protest against governmental repressions.

60 Dmitrii Nikolaevich Ovsianiko-Kulikovskii, 1853–1920, well-known professor and philologist and editor of the journal *Vestnik Evropy* (Herald of Europe).

61 Maksim Moiseevich Vinaver, 1863–1926, member of the Constitutional Democratic Party, organized the League of Philosemites to enlist public support against pogroms.

62 Fëdor Kuz'mich Sologub (real name, Teternikov), 1863–1927, a well-known writer and poet of the modernist-symbolist group.

NOTE TO LETTER 68

63 See Letter 67, note 62.

NOTES TO LETTER 69

64 Sologub; see Letter 67, note 62.

65 K. K. Arsen'ev, 1837–1919, influential liberal publicist.

66 See Letter 67, note 60.

67 V. A. Miakotin, b. 1867, historian and publicist, editor-in-chief of *Russian Riches*.

68 This reference could not be identified.

NOTES TO LETTER 70

69 Apparently an unpublished story by Andreev called "The Tsar" (see Letter 53, note 61).

70 See Letter 32, note 44.

71 See Letter 20, note 79.

72 Andreev used the theme of an astronomer in his play *K zvezdam*, (To the Stars), finished November, 1905.

73 The Russo-Japanese War ended August 23, 1905.

NOTES TO LETTER 71

74 Gorky is continuing his argument with Andreev on the story "The Tsar" (see Letter 53, note 61). Andreev may have decided not to publish this story because of Gorky's objections.

75 Ekaterina Pavlovna Volzhina, Gorky's wife, whom he married

in 1896, a nobleman's daughter from Samara, well educated, who worked as a proofreader on the *Samara Gazette* where Gorky was a staff contributor. They were separated in 1904.

76 Gorky had hoped to write a play on this theme. Andreev's play was titled *K zvezdam* (To the Stars); see Letter 70, note 72.

77 Either Iasin or Iasli in the original. Gorky may be referring to Yalta (see Letter 70).

78 See Letter 49.

79 See Letter 10, note 32. Skitalets married the daughter of a rich Siberian merchant.

NOTES TO LETTER 72

80 Piatnitskii; see Letter 17, note 62. The members of *Znanie* may have been preparing a present for him.

81 See Letter 33, note 52.

82 See Letter 29, note 12.

83 See Letter 13, note 44.

84 See Letter 29, note 11.

85 See Letter 10, note 32.

86 S. I. Elpat'evskii; see Letter 49, note 45.

87 Pseudonym for Nikolai Georgievich Mikhailovskii, 1852-1906, writer and engineer.

88 Ivan Alekseevich Belousov, 1863-1930, poet; a tailor by profession.

89 Possibly A. Bogdanovich; see Letter 3, note 7.

90 A humorous name invented by Gorky for publishers who exploit beginning writers.

NOTES TO LETTER 73

91 Piatnitskii; see Letter 17, note 62, and Letter 72.

92 Skitalets; see Letter 10, note 32, and Letter 49, note 48.

93 See Letter 33, note 52.

94 See Letter 29, note 12.

95 See Letter 29, note 11.

96 Possibly Gorky was referring to December 6, the tsar's nameday, often used by the reactionaries as an occasion for excesses, or November 6, 1905, when the last Zemstvo Congress convened at the height of revolutionary disturbances throughout the empire.

97 Andreev's wife.

98 See Letter 13, note 42, and Letter 47.

99 See Letter 58, note 94.

1 Real name, Alekseev; see Letter 62, note 25.

2 Vladimir Ivanovich Nemirovich-Danchenko; see Letter 24, note 94.

3 Probably a reference to Gorky's telegram from Riga (Letter 64).

NOTES TO LETTER 74

4 See Letter 65.

5 Piatnitskii; see Letter 17, note 62.

6 Apparently Andreev wanted to receive his payment for "Red Laugh" in German marks for use abroad.

7 Andreev's wife.

8 Nemirovich-Danchenko; see Letter 24, note 94. Gorky is referring to the failure of the play *U monastyria* (At the Monastery) by the mediocre dramatist P. M. Iartsev, presented by the Moscow Art Theater on December 21, 1904. Gorky and his mistress Andreeva had plans to organize another art theater.

9 Japanese-sounding nonsense words, an allusion to the Russo-Japanese War.

NOTES TO LETTER 75

10 Morozov; see Letter 66, note 52.

11 Ivan Pavlovich Ladyzhnikov, publisher of works by Gorky and other *Znanie* writers in Berlin.

12 Gorky and Andreeva left for the United States in late March, 1906. His purpose was to escape from repressions inside Russia, to conduct a campaign through the press and public lectures against the efforts of the tsarist government to obtain a loan abroad, and to raise money for the Social Democrats.

13 At this time Gorky was openly calling himself a Social Democrat, although he did not mention whether he belonged to the Bolshevik or Menshevik faction.

14 Bernhardt von Bülow, chancellor of Germany, 1900–1909.

15 Andreev's wife; the whole family was living in Berlin.

16 Andreeva; see Letter 59, note 11.

NOTES TO LETTER 76

17 Gorky arrived in New York on April 10, 1906 (N.S.), and stayed at the Hotel Belleclaire until April 14. For an account of Gorky's visit to New York, see Ernest Poole, "Maxim Gorki in New York," *Slavonic and East European Review*, XXII, No. 58 (May, 1944), 77-83.

18 Konstantin Dmitrievich Bal'mont, 1867-1943, popular poet.

NOTES TO LETTER 77

19 Gorky was in the United States from April to October, 1906 (*Daty zhizni M. Gor'kogo*).

20 See Letter 10, note 32.

21 Mark Twain was prepared to greet Gorky on his arrival but under pressure from certain circles, which had in turn been influenced by agents of the Russian government, he was forced to refuse to arrange a special banquet (see Introduction). The scandal was caused by the fact that Gorky was accompanied by his mistress, M. F. Andreeva (see Letter 59, note 11).

22 This apparently is a reference to a painting or a play which could not be identified.

23 Andreev's wife.

NOTES TO LETTER 78

24 A story by Andreev, finished August, 1906.

25 Possibly Ivan Pavlovich Ladyzhnikov; see Letter 75, note 11.

26 A reference to Gorky's novel *Mother*, first written in the United States during the summer of 1906 and published in English in 1907 by D. Appleton and Co., New York. At the time of the letter he was revising it for publication in Russia, where it appeared in *Znanie Literary Volume No. 18* (1907).

27 *Vragi*, a play by Gorky, written in rough draft during his stay in the United States during the summer of 1906.

28 Andreev's wife was expecting the birth of a child. "Lady Shura," as Gorky affectionately called her, died in childbirth, November 28, 1906 (N.S.), in Berlin. Shortly after her death, Andreev joined Gorky in Capri.

29 This reference could not be identified.
30 See Letter 17, note 62.
31 See Letter 53, note 61, also letter 70.

NOTES TO LETTER 79

32 Written shortly after Gorky's arrival in Italy from the United States and before the death of Andreev's wife.

33 *Zhizn' cheloveka*, a play with symbolic characters by Andreev, finished on September 23, 1906.

34 Could not be identified.

35 Could not be identified.

36 Alexander Nikolaevich Afanas'ev, 1826-1871, an ethnographer, folklorist, collector of folk tales, and scholar of old Russian mythology, who explained mythology as a naïve attempt by the people to explain the forces of nature.

37 An affectionate name for Andreev's wife, who died in childbirth in Berlin on November 28, 1906.

NOTES TO LETTER 80

38 Piatnitskii; see Letter 17, note 62.
39 Alexander Aleksandrovich Blok, 1880-1921, symbolist poet.
40 See Letter 67, note 62.
41 Sergei Abramovich Auslander, 1866-1922(?), minor writer.
42 Aleksei Ivanovich Somov, 1869-1939(?), writer and artist, who specialized in reviving eighteenth-century genres, a modernist.

43 Boris Konstantinovich Zaitsev, b. 1881, a beginning writer at that time, subsequently one of the first rank *émigré* authors.

44 Vasilii Vasil'evich Bashkin, 1880-1909, poet and writer.

45 Viktor Vasil'evich Muizhel', a writer whose works first appeared in 1904.

46 Sergei Nikolaevich Sergeev-Tsenskii, writer.
47 Could not be identified.
48 Leonid Semënov, poet and writer.
49 Andreev bought a piece of land and built a house in Finland in late 1907 (see Vadim Andreev, "Povest' ob ottse," *Russkie zapiski* (Paris), May-December, 1938, and *Literaturnoe nasledstvo*, No. 2 (1932), 104-8).

50 *Severnye al'manakhi, Belye nochi,* and *Vesy* were all modernist publications.

NOTES TO LETTER 81

51 Probably follows Letter 80. Published in *Literaturnoe nasledstvo,* No. 2 (1932), 105-8.

52 "T'ma," a story by Andreev, written in 1907, which gave an unfavorable interpretation of a revolutionary.

53 "Proklatie zveria," published 1907.

54 See Letter 53, note 61.

55 See Letter 79, note 37.

56 From November, 1906, until the spring of 1907, Andreev was on Capri with Gorky.

57 See Letter 80, note 49.

58 See Letter 65, note 49.

NOTES TO LETTER 82

59 This letter is probably a reply to Andreev's letter of February 11, 1908 (Letter 81). Andreev's reply to Gorky follows (Letter 83).

60 See Letter 33, note 51.

61 Zinaida Nikolaevna Hippius, 1869-1945, sometimes writing under the name "Anton Krainii," Merezhkovskii's wife and an important contributor to the modernist journals *New Path* and *The Scales.* She wrote an article "Notes sur la littérature russe de notre temps," sharply criticizing Andreev in *Mercure de France,* LXXI (Jan.-Feb., 1908), 71-79.

62 *Vesy* (The Scales); see Letter 47, note 20, and Letter 54, note 72.

63 See Letter 55, note 76. Kuprin wrote the short story "Izumrud" (The Emerald) in 1908 and in the same year published "Sulamith," a stylized work based on Solomon's "Song of Songs" and bordering on pornography.

64 A reference to Sologub's quasi-pornographic tendencies (see Letter 67, note 62).

65 See Letter 81, note 52.

66 Arkadii Georgievich Gornfel'd, critic and scholar who opposed materialism.

67 *Nav'i chary* (Fairy Magic), a novel by F. Sologub, published by *Shipovnik* in 1908.

NOTES TO LETTER 83

68 Follows Letter 82. Published in *Literaturnoe nasledstvo*, No. 2 (1932), 108-12. Gorky apparently never answered this letter (see Letter 85).

69 See Letter 81, note 52.

70 See Letter 53, note 61.

71 *Savva (Ignis Sanat)*, a play by Andreev published in Stuttgart in 1906.

72 "Judas Iscariot" ("Iskariot"), a story by Andreev, written in 1907.

73 *Shipovnik*, a publishing house, which published primarily the modernists and symbolists. After February, 1907, Andreev became an editor of the *Shipovnik* almanacs of creative literature. Volumes V-VII of his collected works were published by *Shipovnik*; volumes I-IV had been published by *Znanie*.

74 See Letter 17, note 62.

75 *Nav'i chary*, published in the *Shipovnik Almanac* of 1908; Andreev was one of the editors. See Letter 82, note 67.

76 See Letter 80, note 39.

77 See Letter 47, note 20.

78 See Letter 29, note 12.

79 "Rasskaz o semi poveshennykh," dedicated to Leo Tolstoy, finished in late March, 1908.

80 A reference to the attacks on Andreev in *The Decay of Literature* series, of which Gorky was a sponsor.

81 See Letter 54, note 72.

82 See Letter 33, note 51.

83 See Letter 55, note 76.

84 See Letter 82, note 61.

85 Anatolii Vasil'evich Lunacharskii, 1875-1933, a Social Democrat, subsequently an eminent Bolshevik and People's Commissar for Education. In 1908 he wrote an article sharply criticizing Andreev's "Darkness" which was published in *The Decay of Literature* series and which labelled Andreev "the gravedigger of the revolution."

86 See Letter 33, note 49.

87 P. V. Burenin, who wrote about Andreev in the official journal *New Times*.

88 See Letter 82.

89 A. P. Kamenskii, a writer, author of the pornographic novel *Leda*.

90 *Russkii listok*, a sensational newspaper. N. L. Kozetskii was editor after 1898.

91 A reference to a she-goat which appears in a frequently quoted and parodied poem by Briusov.

92 Pseudonym for L. L. Kobylinskii, symbolist poet and theoretician and contributor to *The Scales*.

93 Mikhail Alekseevich Kuzmin, 1875-1936 (?), modernist poet.

94 N. A. Feofilaktov, illustrator for *The Scales*.

95 Pseudonym of Leonid Gabrilovich, feature writer for the Cadet journal *Rech'* (Speech), an organ of the Constitutional Democratic Party, to which modernists contributed. It was very hostile to Andreev.

96 The Party of Peaceful Reform (Mirnoe obnovlenie), a group of Octobrists and Cadets, publishers of the journal *Moscow Weekly*. An article by Filosofov attacking Andreev appeared in the March 18, 1908, issue.

NOTES TO LETTER 84

97 Halley's comet, mentioned in this letter, could be seen in Europe from the end of 1909 to the end of 1910.

98 It had been proposed that Andreev become an editor of the *Znanie* volumes.

99 Piatnitskii; see Letter 17, note 62.

1 See Letter 82, note 61.

2 See Letter 83, note 93.

3 See Letter 80, note 39. *Stikhi o prekrasnoi dame* (Poems about the Beautiful Lady), 1904, *Balaganchik* (The Showman), 1907, and *Neznakomka* (The Stranger), 1907.

4 A loosely organized movement for reform and revolution of the last half of the nineteenth century, much of which was directed toward reforming the government by developing the social consciousness of the peasants. The movement lacked a unified concrete ideology. Its twentieth-century successors were the Socialist Revolutionaries.

5 "Shpion," a story by Gorky which was first published abroad in translation. The Russian original is called "Zhizn' nenuzhnogo cheloveka" (Life of an Unnecessary Man).

6 Apparently a reference to "The Tsar"; see Letter 53, note 61.

7 Andreev's play *Zhizn' cheloveka* (Life of Man). See Letter 79.

8 See Letter 83, note 95.

NOTES TO LETTER 85

9 Published in *M. Gor'kii: materialy i issledovaniia*, I, 141-45. The letter is typewritten, except for the last phrase, the signature, and the date.

10 Engineer and writer.

11 See Letter 17, note 62.

12 See Letter 83, note 85.

13 See Letter 2, note 4. *Sovremennik* (The Contemporary) was a journal in which Gorky participated for a short interval (Autumn, 1912, to May, 1913) while he endeavored to reorganize it in accordance with his own views.

NOTES TO LETTER 86

14 Before Gorky joined the editorial staff of *The Contemporary* for a brief period in the autumn of 1912.

This letter was published in the USSR in *M. Gor'kii: materialy i issledovaniia*, I, 145-50; it is an answer to Letter 85. Andreev's answer, Letter 87, follows.

The footnote to this letter in the Soviet edition states that the section of Gorky's letter beginning with the words "Already the former supporters of 'pure art' . . ." and ending ". . . all these profundities nose to nose" was crossed out in red pencil on the typed copy retained in Gorky's files, leading the editor to assume that Gorky had removed that part of the letter from the copy he sent Andreev; actually the complete passage does appear in the letter Andreev received.

15 See Letter 81, note 52.

16 "Moi zapiski," an article by Andreev, finished September 13, 1908.

17 Georgii Ivanovich Chulkov, writer. At first he was associated with the Social Democrats and was exiled; later he joined the modernists. He preached a doctrine of mystical anarchism (see his memoirs, *Gody stranstvovanii*, [Moscow, 1930]). In 1906 and 1907 he edited the *Fakel* volumes, where Andreev's story "Tak bylo" (So It Was) was first published.

18 See Letter 33, note 51.

19 Kornei Chukovskii, a critic who wrote a great deal about Andreev (e.g., *Leonid Andreev bol'shoi i malen'kii* [St. Petersburg, T-vo "Izdatel'skoe biuro," 1908]).

20 See Letter 55, note 76.

21 Ieronim Ieronimovich Iasinskii (pseudonym, Irinarkh Plutarkhov), 1850-1931, had been a reactionary since 1870 but from time to time changed his position. He joined the Communist Party after the Revolution. Gorky despised him and in early October, 1911, he refused to continue his connections with *New Life* because Iasinskii was a participant.

22 See Letter 83, note 85.

23 See Letter 17, note 62. Piatnitskii disillusioned Gorky by publishing works hostile to revolution. Gorky had opposed *Znanie* since 1911.

24 One of the shareholders in the *Shipovnik* publishing house; see Letter 83, note 73.

25 See Letter 47, note 20.

26 This writer's congress apparently did not take place.

27 See Letter 85, note 13.

NOTES TO LETTER 87

28 Answer to Letter 86. Published in *M. Gor'kii: materialy i issledovaniia*, I, 151. The whole letter is in Andreev's handwriting.

29 See Letter 81, note 52.

30 See Letter 86, note 16.

NOTES TO LETTER 88

31 This letter has been published in *M. Gor'kii: materialy i issledovaniia*, I, 151-52. It is in answer to Letter 87. The letter is dated exactly in the Soviet edition although there was no date on the letter Andreev received. Gorky must have dated the copy which he retained.

32 Gorky was waiting for Andreev's story *Sashka Zhegulëv*, which Andreev had mentioned in his letter (87) to Gorky.

33 Tolstoy's play *Zhivoi trup*, published and staged after the writer's death, led to much controversy in the press.

NOTES TO LETTER 89

34 Published in *M. Gor'kii: materialy i issledovaniia*, I, 173-75. The letter is typewritten, with the section beginning "Life is so disturbing . . ." to the end added in pencil.

35 See Letter 56, note 83.

36 Andreev's first wife.

37 See Letter 88, note 32.

38 A. A. Izmailov, 1873-1921, literary critic.

NOTES TO LETTER 90

39 This letter was published in the USSR in *M. Gor'kii: materialy i issledovaniia*, I, 154-57. The letter was typewritten and undated. This is a reply to Andreev's letter (89), also undated.

40 See Letter 88, note 32. *Sashka Zhegulëv* was finished in October, 1911.

41 City in northern European Russia where political offenders were sent.

42 Andreev's first wife, who died in 1906.

43 The last two sentences were written in by hand, not typewritten.

NOTES TO LETTER 91

44 Reply to Letter 90. Published in *M. Gor'kii: materialy i issledovaniia*, I, 157-65. Typewritten except for the end, beginning with the words, "If I give you pain . . ." which is added by hand. Emphasis apparently Andreev's throughout.

45 See Letter 55, note 76.

46 *Peterburgskaia gazeta*, a sensational newspaper with a reactionary editorial policy.

47 *Sinii zhurnal*, a sensational weekly.

48 See Letter 33, note 51.

49 Peasant hero of Korolenko's *Makar's Dream*, who is allowed into heaven despite his sins because his sufferings have been heavy.

50 See Letter 33, note 49.

51 A. V. Amfiteatrov, 1862-1923, organized in 1911 *The Contemporary*, which he left in 1912; he was replaced by Evgenii Aleksandrovich Liatskii (see Letter 98, note 57). The *Krasnoe znamia* (Red

Banner) was a political and literary monthly published in 1906. Only six issues appeared.

52 See Letter 53, note 61.

53 See Letter 83, note 79.

54 *Chernye maski*, a play by Andreev, 1908.

55 See Letter 86, note 16.

56 See Letter 81, note 52.

57 See Letter 30, note 24.

58 See Letter 89, note 38.

59 See Letter 88, note 32.

60 See Letter 82, note 61.

61 A. E. Red'ko, 1866–1933, critic.

62 See Letter 86, note 21.

63 A. E. Gruzinskii, outstanding literary scholar and critic.

64 *Kon' blednyi*, a novel by Ropshin (pseudonym for V. Savinkov, revolutionary terrorist) published in 1909.

65 D. V. Filosofov, b. 1872, critic and colleague of Merezhkovskii's on *New Path*; see Letter 59, note 6.

66 Konstantin Ivanovich Arabazhin, literary critic.

67 See Letter 83, note 72.

68 *Russkoe slovo*, a Moscow daily, moderate in its political views. Gorky's article had been called "On the Present Day."

69 See Letter 80, note 39, and Letter 84, note 3.

70 See Letter 67, note 62.

71 *Vekhi*, a literary almanac.

72 I. A. Rodionov, author of an extremely conservative work on the peasant, published in 1909.

NOTES TO LETTER 92

73 This letter was published in the USSR in *M. Gor'kii: materialy i issledovaniia*, I, 166–67. It was typewritten. Although the copy retained in Gorky's files was apparently undated, the original which Andreev received had the date added by hand. It is in reply to Letter 91.

74 See Letter 90.

75 See Letter 54, note 71, and Letter 59, note 5.

76 "O sovremennosti," article by Gorky published in January, 1912, in *Russkoe slovo*, Nos. 51 and 52.

77 Vladimir Sergeevich Solov'ëv, 1853–1900, idealist philosopher, theologian, and poet.

78 See Letter 33, note 50.

79 "Judas Iscariot"; see Letter 83, note 72.

80 A. Roslavlev, poet. Gorky mentions him in his article in *Kniga o Leonide Andreeve* (Petrograd: Izd. Z. I. Grzhebina, 1922) p. 31.

81 Could not be identified.

82 N. Golovanov, translator of poetry and Moscow bookseller.

83 See Letter 80, note 39.

84 See Letter 17, note 62, and Letter 86, note 23.

85 See Letter 2, note 4. Gorky had withdrawn from *Znanie* in 1910 and he also left *Legacy* in 1912 because it published a novel by Ropshin-Savinkov, *To, chego ne bylo* (That Which Has Not Been) against Gorky's wishes.

86 Gorky and Shaliapin were friends at first (see Letter 20). They split after Shaliapin publicly announced his sincere devotion to the tsar shortly after the outbreak of the war, during the presentation of an opera.

87 See Letter 86, note 21.

88 After this phrase, the remainder of the letter was added by hand.

NOTES TO LETTER 93

89 Follows Letter 92. Published in *M. Gor'kii: materialy i issledovaniia*, I, 168-70. Typewritten except for the final section starting "Next winter in November . . ." which is added by hand.

90 See Letter 83, note 72.

91 See Letter 81, note 52.

92 See Letter 86, note 16.

93 See Letter 20, note 81, and Letter 92.

94 See Letter 33, note 50.

95 These words were underlined in blue pencil, probably by Gorky, not Andreev.

NOTES TO LETTER 94

96 This letter was published in the USSR in *M. Gor'kii: materialy i issledovaniia*, I, 170. Typewritten and undated. The copy in Gorky's files apparently ended with the sentence about Strindberg. This is a reply to Andreev's letter (93).

97 Referring to the death of the Swedish playwright August Strindberg, 1912.

98 The remainder of the letter was added by hand.

99 *Mody i dzhentl'men*, a journal. Gorky was hostile to Professors Batiushkov and E. V. Anichkov, although he had corresponded with Batiushkov at one time.

NOTES TO LETTER 95

1 Follows Letter 94. Published in *M. Gor'kii: materialy i issledovaniia*, I, 171-72. Typewritten except for the last sentence.

2 See Letter 59, note 11.

3 See Letter 94, note 99.

4 See Letter 83, note 89.

5 See Letter 33, note 49.

6 Famous restaurant in St. Petersburg.

7 A journal with Socialist-Revolutionary tendencies. Edited by V. S. Miroliubov from 1912 to 1914.

8 See Letter 85, note 13.

9 Traditional title of the carters of Orël province, who were famous fistfighters.

10 Author of the novel *Pale Horse*; see Letter 91, note 64, and Letter 92, note 85.

11 See Letter 82, note 61.

12 A. S. Izgoev, pseudonym for A. S. Lande, a journalist who worked for *Russian Thought* from 1908 to 1913.

13 Pseudonym for Ivan Egorovich Vol'nov, writer.

14 See Letter 88, note 32.

15 See Letter 33, note 51.

16 See Letter 47, note 20.

17 Razumnik Vasil'evich Ivanov-Razumnik, 1878-1946, critic and sociologist. A Socialist Revolutionary.

18 The workers in the Siberian goldfields on the Lena River went on strike in February, 1912, because of unbearable conditions and low pay. The troops were called in to break up the strike; on April 4 they shot into the crowd of strikers, wounding 250 and killing 270. The liberals were deeply aroused by these events; Andreev wrote Gorky in order to request that he contribute to a volume that a group of writers were publishing for the benefit of the Lena workers who had suffered during the uprising. The volume was never published.

19 See Letter 32, note 42.

20 Andreev was one of the editors of the almanacs of creative literature published by *Shipovnik*. V. E. Kopel'man was an associate of the publishing company.

NOTES TO LETTER 96

21 A reply to Andreev's letter (95).

22 See Letter 95, note 13.

23 Pseudonym for V. Savinkov; see Letter 91, note 64, and Letter 92, note 85.

24 Vladimir Kirillovich Vinnichenko, Ukrainian writer, also popular in Russia.

25 Sholom Asch, writer in Russian and Yiddish.

26 Pseudonym for Akim L'vovich Flekser, b. 1863, ideologist of literary modernism.

27 See Letter 13, note 44.

28 Pseudonym for Osip I. Perel'man, writer and dramatist.

29 Could not be identified.

30 Popular romantic actor in the Aleksandrinskii Theater in St. Petersburg.

31 See Letter 65, note 49.

32 See Letter 55, note 76.

33 F. Sologub; see Letter 67, note 62.

34 See Letter 33, note 51.

35 See Letter 95, note 18.

36 Il'ia Dmitrievich Surguchev, b. 1881, writer and dramatist.

37 Aleksei Zolotarev, Rybinsk writer, expelled from Russia for "unreliability." He lived in Capri for a while.

38 See Letter 94, note 99.

39 See Letter 95, note 20.

40 Translated into Russian in 1906 and 1907.

41 K. F. Zhakov, 1865–1926, a Ziranian who wrote in Russian, an ethnographer and philosopher.

NOTES TO LETTER 97

42 Follows Letter 96. Published in *M. Gor'kii: materialy i issledovaniia*, I, 152–53. Typewritten except for last phrase.

Although the date "15 November 1911" is written on the letter, specific references, the general tone, and the sequence of letters suggest that 1911 was written in error for 1912.

43 Ladyzhnikov; see Letter 75, note 11.

44 See Letter 83, note 73, and Letter 86, note 24.

45 See Letter 96.

NOTES TO LETTER 98

46 A reply to Letter 97.

47 The *Shipovnik* edition; see Letter 96.

48 Gorky's satirical name for V. S. Miroliubov (see Letter 2, note 4, and Letter 95, note 7.)

49 Gorky calls *Legacy* "Muir and Merilees" in reference to the big general store in Moscow of that name resembling Woolworth's; see Letter 95, note 7.

50 See Letter 33, note 61.

51 Perhaps V. M. Chernov, 1873-1932, a Socialist Revolutionary leader.

52 See Letter 95, note 17.

53 Sergei Dmitrievich Mstislavskii, b. 1879, Socialist Revolutionary.

54 *Professor Storitsyn*, a play by Andreev, 1912.

55 *Ekaterina Ivanovna*, a play by Andreev, 1912.

56 V. L'vov-Rogachevskii, 1874-1930, Marxist critic.

57 Evgenii Aleksandrovich Liatskii, critic and one of the leaders of the journal *The Contemporary* (see Letter 91, note 51). Gorky, who was invited by Liatskii, attempted to reorganize the journal in accordance with his own ideas from the autumn of 1912 to May, 1913.

NOTES TO LETTER 99

58 Answers Letter 98. Published in *M. Gor'kii: materialy i issledovaniia*, I, 153-54.

59 See Letter 96.

60 See Letter 70, note 72.

61 See Letter 32, note 44.

62 See Letter 60, note 16.

63 A story by Andreev, published 1909.

64 See Letter 83, note 79.

65 A play by Andreev, published 1909.

66 Heroine of *Ekaterina Ivanovna*; see Letter 98, note 55.

67 See Letter 24, note 94.

68 See Letter 19, note 68.

69 See Letter 98, note 48.

70 See Letter 13, note 44.

71 See Letter 14, note 50.

NOTE TO LETTER 100

72 This letter does not refer to any letter in the Gorky collection. It was probably written in 1913, when Gorky was arranging to return to Russia, although the original contains a penciled note by Gorky: "Probably 1914." Published in *M. Gor'kii: materialy i issledovaniia*, I, 176.

NOTES TO LETTER 101

73 The original of this letter to Andreev does not exist in the collection of Gorky's letters to Andreev at the Columbia University Libraries. It comes from the Gorky Archive in the Saltykov-Shchedrin State Public Library in Leningrad and was published in *M. Gor'kii: materialy i issledovaniia*, I, 176-78. Typewritten.

74 The letter discusses Andreev's play, *Samson in Chains*, written in 1914.

75 See Letter 32, note 44.

76 Possibly Galial, an important character in *Samson in Chains*.

SELECTED BIBLIOGRAPHY

REFERENCE WORKS

Bol'shaia sovetskaia entsiklopediia (Large Soviet Encyclopedia). 1st ed., 65 vols. Moscow, Gos. Izd. "BSE," 1926-47. 2nd ed., 30 vols. (to letter "O"). Moscow, Gos. Izd. "BSE," 1949-53.

Entsiklopedicheskii slovar' Brokgauza i Efrona (Brockhaus and Efron Encyclopedic Dictionary). 82 vols. and 4 supps. St. Petersburg, Izd. Brokgauza-Efrona, 1890-1906. *Novyi entsiklopedicheskii slovar' Brokgauza i Efrona* (New Brockhaus and Efron Encyclopedic Dictionary). 29 vols. (to letter "O"). St. Petersburg, Izd. Brokgauza-Efrona, 1911-16.

Entsiklopedicheskii slovar' "Granat" (Granat Encyclopedic Dictionary). 7th ed., 52 vols. Moscow, Izd. "Brat'ev A. i I. Granat i Co.," 1909-34.

Literaturnaia entsiklopediia (Literary Encyclopedia). Moscow, Izd. "Kommunisticheskoi Akademii," 1929-39. Vols. I-IX, XI.

MASANOV, I. F. *Biograficheskii slovar' psevdonimov russkikh pisatelei* (Biographical Dictionary of Pseudonyms of Russian Writers). Moscow, Izd. "Vsesoiuznoi knizhnoi palaty." Vol. I, 1941. Vols. II and III, 1949.

VENGEROV, A. S. *Kritiko-biograficheskii slovar'* (Critical-Biographical Dictionary). Petrograd, Izd. "Tovarishchestvo khudozhestvennoi pechati," 1915-16. Vols. I and II.

GORKY AND ANDREEV

ALEXINSKY, G. *La vie amère de Maxime Gorki.* Grenoble, B. Arthaud, 1950.

"*Daty zhizni i deiatel'nosti A. M. Gor'kogo (preimushchestvenno po materialam Departamenta Politsii)*" (Dates in the Life and Activity of A. M. Gorky [Primarily Based on Police Department Files]),

Krasnyi arkhiv (Red Archives), LXXVIII (1936), 23-84. In the footnotes this source is abbreviated as *Daty zhizni M. Gor'kogo.*

"Dva pis'ma L. Andreeva k M. Gor'komu" (Two Letters from Andreev to Gorky), *Literaturnoe nasledstvo* (Literary Heritage), No. 2 (1932), pp. 105-16.

FATOV, N. N. *Molodye gody Leonida Andreeva* (The Young Years of Leonid Andreev). Moscow, Izd. "Zemlia i fabrika," 1924.

FERRETTI, G. "M. Gor'kij o il puro artista come rivoluzionario," in *Atti della Reale Accademia di scienze, lettere e arti di Palermo,* 1949, Ser. 4, VIII, Pt. 2, 173-240.

GORKI, M. "More Reminiscences of L. Andreyev," *Dublin Magazine,* III (1925), 1-8. Authorized translation from the Russian.

—— *Reminiscences of Tolstoy, Chekhov, Andreyev.* New York, Dover, 1946.

GRUZDEV, I. *Gor'kii i ego vremia* (Gorky and His Time). Moscow, Gos. Izd. khudozhestvennoi literatury, 1938. Vol. I.

KAUN, A. *L. Andreyev, a Critical Study.* New York, Huebsch, 1924.

—— *Maxim Gorky and His Russia.* New York, Cape and Smith, 1931.

M. Gor'kii: materialy i issledovaniia (M. Gorky: Materials and Research). Edited by V. A. Desnitskii and S. D. Balukhatyi. Leningrad, Institute of Russian Literature, Academy of Sciences, USSR. Vol. I, 1934. Vol. II, 1937. Vol. III, 1941 (actually published 1945).

RUDNEV, V. *Gor'kii-revoliutsioner* (Gorky the Revolutionary). Moscow-Leningrad, Gos. Izd., 1929.

TSENTROARKHIV. *Revoliutsionnyi put' M. Gor'kogo (po materialam Departamenta Politsii)* (Central Archives. The Revolutionary Road of Maxim Gorky [from Police Department Files]). Edited by E. Iaroslavskii. Moscow-Leningrad, Gos. Izd. khudozhestvennoi literatury, 1933.

VOLKOV, A. A. *M. Gor'kii i literaturnoe dvizhenie kontsa 19 i nachala 20-go veka* (M. Gorky and the Literary Movement of the End of the Nineteenth and the Beginning of the Twentieth Centuries). Moscow, Izd. "Sovetskii pisatel'," 1951.

WOLF, F. *Maxim Gorki, revolutionärer Romantiker und sozialistischer Realist.* Berlin, Henscheverlag, 1953.

INDEX

"Abyss, The" (Andreev), 34, 40, 46, 159
Academy of Science (St. Petersburg), 141
Afanas'ev, Alexander Nikolaevich, 92, 177
"Alarm" (Andreev), 34, 38, 40, 158
Aleksandrinskii Theater (St. Petersburg), 187
Alekseev, Sergei Aleksandrovich (pseud. Naidenov), 6, 67, 82, 169
Alekseevskii, Arkadii Pavlovich, 24, 47, 48, 81, 152
Aleksin, Alexander, 41, 44, 53, 162
Alexander II, Emperor, 4
Alexinsky, Gregoire, 3, 9n
Amfiteatrov, A. V., 124, 183
Anathema (Andreev), 8, 142, 188
Andreev, Leonid Nikolaevich, 3-13
Andreev, Vadim, 47, 48, 163-64
Andreeva, Mar'ia Fëdorovna (also called Maruska; Marusia), 64, 68, 70, 74, 85, 136, 169, 175, 176
Andreevich (pseud. of Evgenii Andreevich Solov'ëv), 19, 20, 44, 150
"Anfisa" (Andreev), 142, 188
Anichkov, E. V., 13, 136, 186
Annenskii, Innokentii Fëdorovich, 49, 165
Arabazhin, Konstantin Ivanovich, 127, 129, 184
"Arise and Walk" (Andreev; published as "The Life of Vasilii Fiveiskii"), 36, 77, 160
Arsen'ev, K. K., 76, 173
"Artist, The" (Gorky), 105
Artsybashev, M. P., 72, 96, 97, 138, 166, 172
Arzamas, 29, 30, 42, 154, 156
Asch, Sholom, 138
Asheshov, Nikolai Petrovich, 17, 48, 73, 149
Ashkinazi, Vladimir Aleksandrovich (pseud. Pek), 21, 151
"Astronomer, The" (Andreev), see To the Stars
At the Monastery (Iartsev), 83, 175

Auslander, Sergei Abramovich, 93, 177
Avdotia's Life (Alekseev), 67, 82, 170
Avvakum (Old Believer priest), 49, 165

Bal'mont, Konstantin Dmitrievich, 85, 176
Barbara (The Summer Folk), 132
"Bargamot and Garaska" (Andreev), 18, 19, 20, 150; called "The Hippopotamus and the Batman," 151
Bashkin, Vasilii Vasil'evich, 94, 177
Basil the Beatified, Cathedral of (Moscow), 49, 164
Batiushkov, Professor, 13, 136, 137, 139, 186
Beethoven, Ludwig van, 65
Belleclaire, Hotel (N.Y.C.), 85, 176
Belousov, Ivan Alekseevich, 80, 174
Benois, Alexander Nikolaevich, 48, 164
"Ben-Tobit" (Andreev), 166
Berlin, 84, 175, 176
"Bewitched Streetlamp, The" (Ganeizer), 35, 159
Bezobrazov (Byzantine scholar), 13, 29, 155
Bezrodnaia, Julia (pseud. of Juliia Ivanovna Iakovleva), 35, 159
Black Hundreds, 100, 101, 129
Black Maskers (Andreev), 8, 125, 184
Blok, Alexander Aleksandrovich, 93, 94, 99, 105, 129, 132, 177
Blue Journal (weekly), 123, 183
Blumenberg (publisher), 140
Boborykin, Pëtr Dmitrievich, 49, 165
Bogdanovich, A., 36, 80, 150
Bogucharskii, Vasilii Iakovlevich, 38, 161
Bolshevik Party, 4n
Braliantov (writer), 46, 163
Briusov, Valerii Iakovlevich, 48, 98, 100, 102, 114, 137, 164, 167, 180
Brusianin, Vasilii Vasilievich, 29, 30, 156
Bugrov, Old Believer, 153
Bülow, Bernhardt von, 84

INDEX

Bunin, Ivan Alekseevich, 6, 33, 57, 63, 67, 80, 81, 158
Burenin, P. V., 102, 179
"Burevestnik" (Gorky), 154

Cadets (political party), 4n, 100, 103
Capri, 7, 13, 89, 92, 96, 100, 116, 129, 176, 178
Cathedral of Basil the Beatified, 49, 164
Cellini, Benvenuto, 38
"Cemetery, The" (Braliantov), 46
Charcot, Jean Martin, 58
Chekhov, Anton Pavlovich, 18, 21, 50, 56-57, 58, 62, 65, 67, 72, 73, 159, 167, 168
Chernov, V. M., 141, 188
Children of Vaniushin (Alekseev), 170
Chirikov, Evgenii N. (also called Zhenichka), 6, 24, 38, 49, 50, 62, 67, 73, 80, 138, 142, 153
"Christians, The" (Andreev), 21, 152
Chukovskii, Kornei, 112, 182
Chulkov, Georgii Ivanovich, 111, 181
Citizen (newspaper), 160
"City of the Yellow Devil, The" (Gorky), 12
Constitutional Democratic Party, 4n
Contemporary, The (periodical), 110, 114, 137, 149, 181, 183, 188
Contemporary World (periodical), 167
Courier, The (newspaper), 5, 10, 19, 23, 24, 25, 27, 30, 31, 35, 47, 50, 68, 73, 149, 150, 151, 159
Crimea, 13, 56, 156, 157-58
"Curse of the Beast, The" (Andreev), 95, 178

"Darkness" (Andreev), 8, 12, 95, 98, 99, 111, 112, 115, 125, 129, 135, 178, 179
Deaconess Alexandra, *see* Veligor-skaia, Alexandra Mikhailovna
"Death of Landé" (Artsybashev), 72, 172
Decay of Literature, The, 100, 102, 179
Delilah (*Samson in Chains*), 145
"Delusions of Grandeur" (Filosofov), 127
Desnitskii, V. A., 3n

Diaghilev, S. P., 63, 169
Diffenbakh (artist), 91
Dobroliubov, M. A., 49, 165
Donon (restaurant), 137, 186
Doroshevich, Vasilii M., 48, 164
Dostoevsky, Fëdor, 120, 128, 130, 132
Duel, The (Kuprin), 57
Dymov (pseud. of Osip I. Perel'man), 138, 187

Ecclesiastes, 78
Ekaterina Ivanovna (Andreev), 141, 188
Ellis (pseud. of L. L. Kobylinskii), 102, 180
Elpat'evskii, Sergei Iakovlevich, 49, 80, 165
"Emerald, The" (Kuprin), 98, 178
Enemies (Gorky), 90, 176
Engelhardt, N. A., 59, 168
Ermolaev, M. S., 150
"Event, The" (Andreev), 35, 159
Exchange Herald (newspaper), 20, 150
Extinct Monsters (Hutchinson), 87, 168

Fagin, L. A., 24, 31, 35, 38, 40, 149
Fairy Magic (Sologub), 99, 178, 179
Fakel (ed. Chulkov), 181
Farnese Collection (Naples), 89
Feigin, L. A., *see* Fagin, L. A.
Feofilaktov, M. A., 102, 180
Filippov (poet), 25, 154
Filosofov, Dmitri Vladimirovich, 63, 127, 169, 180, 184
Finland, 3, 94, 96, 172, 177
First of March (Iasinskii), 113
Flaubert, Gustave, 77, 90
Flekser, Akim L'vovich (pseud. Volynskii), 138, 187
"For a Moment" (Andreev), 166
"Foreigner, The" (Andreev), 48; *see also* "Student, The"

Gabrilovich, Leonid (pseud. Galich), 103, 180
Galich (pseud. of Leonid Gabrilo-vich), 103, 180
Ganeizer, E., 35, 159
Garin (pseud. of Nikolai Georgievich Mikhailovskii), 80, 174
Gavrilych, *see* Skitalets
"Gendarme, The" (Andreev), 68

194

Ghosts (Ibsen), 74, 172
Giurdzhan (sculptor), 75
God's World (periodical), 5, 17, 36, 150, 159, 161
Goethals, G. W., 87
Gogol, N. V., 127
Golovanov, N., 132, 185
Gol'tsev, Viktor Aleksandrovich, 13, 22, 25, 72, 152
Good in the Teachings of Tolstoy and Nietzsche (Shestov), 38
Gorky, Maxim (pseud. of Aleksei Maksimovich Peshkov), 3 - 13; verses, 54, 55, 167
Gornfel'd, Arkadii Georgievich, 99, 178
"Governor, The" (Andreev), 166
Grammar of Science (Pearson), 139, 187
Grieg, Edvard, 89
Grinevitskii, Stanislav Ivanovich, 31, 32
Gringmut, Vladimir Andreevich, 37, 160
Gruzinskii, A. E., 127, 184
Gusev-Orenburgskii, Sergei Ivanovich, 67, 171

Halley's comet, 105, 180
Hanna, Mark, 87
Harvard University, 87
Herald of Europe (periodical), 173
Hermitage Theater (Moscow), 151
Hippius, Zinaida Nikolaevna (pseud. Anton Krainii; also called Zinochka), 98, 100, 103, 104, 125, 137, 178
"Hippopotamus and the Batman, The" (Andreev), 151; *see also* "Bargamot and Garaska"
History of the Girondists (Lamartine), 73, 82
House of Preliminary Imprisonment (St. Petersburg), 171
"Husband of Duty" (Kornev), 30
Hutchinson, Henry Neville, 60, 168

"I Cannot Be Silent" (Tolstoy), 125
Iakovleva, Iuliia Ivanovna, (pseud. Julia Bezrodnaia), 35, 159
Iakubov (writer), 47, 164
Iarovitskii, Aleksei Vasil'evich (pseud. Kornev), 30, 34, 35, 156

Iartsev, P. M., 175
Iasinskii, Ieronim Ieronimovich (pseud. Irinarkh Plutarkhov), 113, 126, 133, 182
"In the Basement" (Andreev), 34, 35, 40, 158
"In the Dark Distance" (Andreev), 26, 37, 154
"In the Train" (Iakubov), 47
Indians (American), 87
Institute of Russian Literature, Academy of Sciences (Leningrad), 3n
Internal Affairs, Ministry of, 30
"International League," 139
Iordanskii, Nikolai Ivanovich, 56, 167
Israel, 144
Iuvachev, I. P. (pseud. Ivan Pavlovich Miroliubov), 40, 41, 161
Ivan the Terrible, 72
Ivanov-Razumnik, Razumnik Vasil'evich, 138, 141, 186
Izgoev, A. S. (pseud. of A. S. Lande), 137, 186
Izmailov, A. A., 119, 125, 127, 183

Japan, 56, 77, 167
Jews, 27, 71, 73, 144
Journal for All (periodical), 17, 39, 72, 149, 161, 166, 169, 172
Judah, tribe of, 144
"Judas Iscariot" (Andreev), 99, 129, 132, 133, 134, 179
Judea, 144
Judges, Book of, 143

Kamenskii, A. P., 102, 137, 180
Karamazov, Ivan, 121
Kastorskii, S., 7n
Katerina (*Ekaterina Ivanovna*), 141, 142, 189
Kaufman, Abram Evgenievich, 24, 152
Kazan Cathedral (St. Petersburg), 154
Kerzhentsev, Dr. ("Thought"), 42
Khar'kov, 32, 157
Kiev University, 154
King Hunger (Andreev), 95, 99, 100, 101, 125, 166
Kniga o Leonide Andreeve (Gorky), 185
Kobylinskii, L. L. (pseud. Ellis), 102, 180

Kopel'man, V. E., 138, 139, 187
Koreiz, 32
Kornev (pseud. of Aleksei Vasil'-
  evich Iarovitskii), 30, 34, 35, 156
Korolenko, Vladimir Galaktionovich,
  36, 49, 138, 160, 168, 183
Kosorotov, Alexander Ivanovich
  (pseud. "Shmel"), 55, 167
Kozetskii, N. L., 102, 180
Krainii, Anton, see Hippius, Zinaida
  Nikolaevna
Kukol'nik, Nestor Vasil'evich, 27, 154
Kukoretkina, Olga, 57
Kulibin, I. P., 49, 165
Kuprin, Alexander Ivanovich, 6, 57,
  63, 67, 98, 99, 100, 113, 123, 138,
  167, 178
Kuropatkin, A. N., 69, 171
"Kusaka" (Andreev), 35, 40, 159
Kuskova, E. D., 9n
Kuzmin, Mikhail Alekseevich, 94, 102,
  104, 105, 180

La vie amère de Maxime Gorki
  (Alexinsky), 9n
Lady Shura, see Veligorskaia, Alex-
  andra Mikhailovna
Ladyzhnikov, Ivan Pavlovich, 84, 89,
  140, 175
Lamartine, A. M. L. de, 73
"Land and Freedom" group, 4n
Lande, A. S. (pseud. A. S. Izgoev),
  137, 186
Landé, Ivan, 72
Landmarks (literary almanac), 130,
  184
"Laughter" (Andreev), 34, 40, 158,
"Lazarus" (Andreev), 12, 88-89, 176
League of Philosemites, 75, 173
Leda (Kamenskii), 180
Legacy (periodical), 137, 149, 185, 186;
  called "Muir and Merilees," 141,
  188
Lena River, 138, 186
Lenin Library, see Rumiantsev
  Museum
Lenin, Nikolai, 7n
Liatskii, Evgenii Aleksandrovich, 141,
  183, 188
"Liberal, The" (Gorky), 63
Lichtenberger, Henri, 26, 38, 154
Life (periodical), 5, 17, 19, 21, 25, 45,
  150, 153, 154, 155, 161

Life of a Superfluous Man (Gorky), 8
"Life of an Unnecessary Man"
  (Gorky), see "Spy, The"
Life of Man, The (Andreev), 8, 12, 91,
  106, 177
"Life of Vasilii Fiveiskii, The"
  (Andreev), see "Arise and Walk"
L'Intruse (Maeterlinck), 92
Literaturnoe nasledstvo, 3n
Little Devil (Sologub), 93
"Little Negro, The," see "Original
  Fellow, An"
Living Corpse, The (Tolstoy), 116, 182
Lower Depths, The (Gorky), 29, 142,
  154, 155
Lunacharskii, Anatolii Vasil'evich, 9n,
  100, 101, 102, 103, 108, 113, 179
Luzhskii, V., 157, 169
L'vov-Rogachevskii, V., 9, 141, 188
Lynch, James (pseud. of Andreev), 35,
  62, 159

M. Gor'kii: materialy i issledovaniia
  (ed. Desnitskii), 3, 7n
Maeterlinck, Maurice, 92
Makar (Makar's Dream), 124, 183
"Man Who Knocks on All Closed
  Doors" (Andreev), 70
"Marseillaise, The" (Andreev), 68, 166
Marseillaise, The (song), 73
Marusia, see Andreeva, Mar'ia
  Fëdorovna
Maruska, see Andreeva, Mar'ia
  Fëdorovna
Marx, Karl, 4n
Maupassant, Guy de, 139, 140, 141, 142
Mediterranean Sea, 92
"Memorial to Pushkin," 21
Menshevik Party, 4n
Men'shikov, Mikhail Osipovich, 37, 160
Mercure de France (periodical), 98, 178
Merezhkovskii, Dmitrii Sergeevich, 35,
  63, 98, 100, 102, 103, 112, 124, 129,
  137, 138, 160, 161, 169, 178, 184
Meshcherskii, Vladimir Petrovich, 37,
  160
Miakotin, V. A., 76, 173
Mikhailovskii, N. K., 36, 38, 155, 158,
  161, 174
Mikhailovskii, Nikolai Georgievich
  (pseud. Garin), 80, 174
Miklashevskii, Mikhail Petrovich
  (pseud. Nevedomskii), 38, 64, 161

Minin (Russian national hero), 49, 165
Miroliubov, Ivan Pavlovich (pseud. of
I. P. Iuvachev), 40, 41, 161
Miroliubov, Viktor Sergeevich (also
called Viktor Mirov; Viktorian
Mirotëkov), 10, 17, 36, 40, 50, 52,
53, 62, 72, 132, 141, 142, 149, 150,
166, 169, 172, 186, 188
"Monster, The" (Gorky), 57
Morning of Russia (newspaper), 152
Morozov, Savva Timofeevich, 73, 74,
83, 172
Moscow, 13, 49, 71, 157, 158, 167, 169,
172
Moscow Art Theater, 49, 82, 151, 156,
157, 169, 175
Moscow Herald (journal), 160
Moscow House of Scholars, 169
Moscow Weekly (periodical), 180
Mother (Gorky), 7n, 8, 90, 176
Mstislavskii, Sergei Dmitrievich, 141,
188
"Muir and Merilees," *see* Legacy
Muizhel', Viktor Vasil'evich, 94, 177
Murav'ëv, M. N., 38, 161
Mustomiaki, 74, 75, 172
"Mutiny on Shipboard" (Andreev),
34, 48, 50, 57, 159
My Confession (Tolstoy), 128
"My Notes" (Andreev), 8, 111, 112,
115, 125, 129, 135, 181

Nachalo (periodical), 38
Naidenov (pseud. of Sergei Aleksand-
rovich Alekseev), 6, 67, 82, 169
Naples, 89
Narodnik movement, 105, 180
"Nechto o Elke" (Gorky), 153
Negroes, 87
Nemirovich-Danchenko, Vladimir
Ivanovich, 13, 31, 82, 83, 142, 156,
175
Nevedomskii (pseud. of Mikhail
Petrovich Miklashevskii), 38, 64
Nevskii Prospect (St. Petersburg), 137
New Life (periodical), 182
New Path (periodical), 6, 52, 54, 166,
169, 184
New Times (periodical), 59, 101, 124,
137, 159, 160, 168, 179
New Word (periodical), 155
New York City, 85, 86, 176
News of the Day (newspaper), 159

Nezlobin's theatre (Riga), 169
Niagara Falls, 87, 92
Nikon, Patriarch, 49, 165
Nizhnii Novgorod, 13, 28, 49, 153,
154, 155-56, 157, 165
Nizhnii Novgorod Anthology, 49, 56,
68, 79, 165
Nizhnii Novgorod News (newspaper),
27, 30, 31, 34, 53, 156
Northern Almanacs, 94, 178
Northern Land (newspaper), 27
Notes of a Writer (Teleshov), 151,
157, 160
"Notes of the Proletariat" (Gorky), 54
"Notes sur la littérature russe de notre
temps" (Hippius), 98, 178
Novgorodtsev, Pavel Ivanovich, 48,
164
Novik, I. D., 149

Ocean, The (Andreev), 125, 159
"On the Present Day" (Gorky), 129,
130, 132, 184
"On the River" (Andreev), 29
"On the Stories of L. Andreev"
(Kornev), 30
"On Water and Land" (Iakubov), 47
"Once upon a Time" (Andreev), 24,
142, 153
Orël, 49, 137, 138, 186
"Original Fellow, An" (Andreev), 45,
59, 163; called "The Little Negro,"
68, 171
Orlenev, P., 74, 172
Ostrogorskii, V. P., 150
Oswald (*Ghosts*), 74, 172
Our Life (newspaper), 62, 63, 71, 81,
168
Ovsianiko-Kulikovskii, Dmitrii Niko-
laevich, 13n, 74, 76, 173
Oyama, Marshal, 72, 83

Pale Horse (Ropshin), 127, 184
Peaceful Reformers (politcial group),
103, 180
Pearson, C., 139, 187
Pek (pseud. of Vladimir Aleksandro-
vich Ashkinazi), 21, 151
People's Freedom, Party of the, 4n
Perel'man, Osip I. (pseud. Dymov),
138, 187
Peshkov, Aleksei Maksimovich, *see*
Gorky, Maxim

Peshkova, E. P., 10, 11
Petersburg Gazette (newspaper), 63, 123, 169, 183
Petersburg Herald (newspaper), 35, 63, 159, 169
"Pet'ka na dache" (Andreev), 34, 40, 159
Petrov, Stepan Gavrilovich, *see* Skitalets
Petty Bourgeois, The (English trans., *The Smug Citizen*; Gorky), 32, 156-57
"Phantoms" (Andreev), 70, 171
Philistines, 144
Philosophy of Nietzsche, The (Lichtenberger), 26
Piatnitskii, K. P., 10, 33, 34, 38, 40, 43, 46, 49, 56, 57, 61, 64, 67, 79, 80, 82, 90, 93, 104, 108, 113, 132, 154, 174, 182
Plutarkhov, Irinarkh (pseud. of Ieronim Ieronimovich Iasinskii), 113, 126, 133, 182
Podol'sk, 158
Poems about the Beautiful Lady (Blok), 105, 180
Poet Lore (Boston periodical), 156, 167
Polner, Tikhon I., 22, 152
Poole, Ernest, 12*n*
Popov, A. S., *see* Serafimovich, A. S.
Popov, Pavel, 132
Popova, O. N., 26, 154
Port Arthur, 71, 172
Posse, V. A., 19, 20, 21, 38, 150, 155
Potapenko, Ignatii Nikolaevich, 64, 169
"Povest ob ottse" (V. Andreev), 163, 177
Pozharskii (Russian national hero), 49, 165
Professor Storitsyn (Andreev), 141, 188
Pushkin, A. S., 49, 165

Razumnik, *see* Ivanov-Razumnik, Razumnik Vasil'evich
Red Banner (periodical), 87, 124, 183
"Red Laugh" (Andreev), 12, 63, 72, 82, 142, 166, 169, 170, 175
Red'ko, A. E., 125, 184
Reminiscences of Tolstoy, Chekhov, Andreyev (Gorky), 9*n*

Revolution (Andreev), 101
Revolution of 1905, 7, 86, 104
Riga, 68, 74, 83, 169, 171
Rodionov, I. A., 130, 184
Romanov, Mikhail Fëdorovich, 165
Ropshin, *see* Savinkov, V.
Roslavlev, A., 132, 185
Rozanov, V., 37, 132, 135, 160
Rumiantsev Museum (now Lenin Library; Moscow), 49, 164
Russia (newspaper), 55, 63, 167
Russian and East European History and Culture, Archive of, Columbia University, 3
Russian Herald (journal), 159
Russian News (newspaper), 102, 180
Russian Riches (periodical), 27, 29, 30, 36, 38, 155, 159, 161, 173
Russian Thought (periodical), 152, 186
Russian Word (periodical), 37, 129, 130, 164, 184
"Russkii chelovek i znamenitost'" (Andreev), 151
Russo-Japanese War, 58-59, 61-62, 77, 167, 173

Sablin, Vladimir, 28, 29, 31, 32, 155, 156
"Saburovo" (Andreev), 19, 20, 150
St. Petersburg, 13, 58, 71, 83, 153, 156, 169, 171, 172
Sakhalin (I. P. Miroliubov), 40, 41
Samara, 149, 174
Samara Gazette (newspaper), 27, 66, 149, 174
Samson (*Samson in Chains*), 143
Samson in Chains (Andreev), 143-45, 189
Sashka Zhegulëv (Andreev), 8, 9, 12, 115, 119, 121, 125, 137, 182-83
Savinkov, V., 127, 137, 138, 184, 185
Savva (Andreev), 99, 179
Scales, The (periodical), 6, 56, 61, 94, 98, 100, 104, 167, 178, 180
Schopenhauer, Arthur, 34
Semënov, Leonid, 94, 177
Serafimovich, A. S. (pseud. of A. S. Popov), 6, 33, 38, 67, 79, 80, 81, 100, 158
Serëzha, *see* Sergei Aleksandrovich, Grand Prince
Sergeev-Tsenskii, Sergei Nikolaevich, 94

Sergei, Aleksandrovich, Grand Prince (called Serëzha), 68, 70, 171
Sestroretsk, 58, 60-61
"Seven Who Were Hanged, The" (Andreev), 100, 125, 142, 179
Shakespeare, William, 18, 27
Shaliapin, F. I., 28, 33, 49, 132, 135, 155, 158, 185
Shatalets, see Skitalets
Shestov, Lëv Issakovich (pseud. of L. I. Shvartsman), 38, 141, 161
Shipovnik (publishing house), 99, 138, 139, 140, 178, 179, 182, 187
Shipovnik Almanac, 99, 179
Shkliar (writer), 40, 161
"Shmel" (pseud. of Alexander Ivanovich Kosorotov), 55, 167
Showman, The (Blok), 105, 180
Shura, Lady, see Veligorskaia, Alexandra Mikhailovna
Shvartsman, L. I. (pseud. Lëv Issakovich Shestov), 38, 141
Skirmunt, S. A., 43, 47, 49, 162
Skitalets (pseud. of Stepan Gavrilovich Petrov; nicknames Shatalets, Gavrilych), 22, 23, 24, 33, 41, 43, 46, 47, 49, 50, 53, 62, 63, 67, 70, 73, 79, 80, 81, 86, 152, 165, 174
Smidovich, V. V. (pseud. Vikentii Vikent'evich Veresaev), 59, 116, 168
Smug Citizen, The (English trans. of The Petty Bourgeois; Gorky), 32, 156-57
Social Democratic Party, 4n, 7, 8, 84, 100, 175
Socialist Revolutionary Party, 4n, 180
"Society for the Defense of Women," 21, 152
"So It Was" (Andreev), 166, 181
Sologub, Fëdor Kuz'mich (pseud. of F. K. Teternikov), 74, 75, 93, 94, 98, 99, 129, 138, 173, 178
Solov'ëv, Evgenii Andreevich (pseud. Andreevich), 19, 20, 44, 150
Solov'ëv, Vladimir Sergeevich, 132, 184
Somov, Aleksei Ivanovich, 93, 177
Son of the Fatherland (newspaper), 62
"Song of Songs" (Solomon), 98, 178
"Song of the Falcon" (Gorky), 7n
Sorin, Savva Abramovich, 47, 164
Spadero (fisherman), 89

Speech (periodical), 106, 180
Speranskii, M. M., 49, 165
"Spy, The" (Russian original, "Life of an Unnecessary Man"; Gorky), 105, 180
Stars (Andreev), 142
Stepan, see Skitalets
"Story about Sergei Petrovich, The" (Andreev), 19, 20, 21, 29, 150, 151, 153
Stössel, A. M., 71, 172
Stranger, The (Blok), 105, 180
Strindberg, August, 136, 137, 185
"Student, The" (Andreev), 34, 159
Styles and the Gentleman (periodical), 136, 137
"Sulamith" (Kuprin), 99, 178
Summer Folk, The (Gorky), 63, 64, 67, 132, 167
Surguchev, Il'ia Dmitrievich, 139, 187

Tararakhtenberg (Vladimir Osipovich Trachtenberg), 55, 167
Teleshov, N. D., 6, 38, 79, 80, 81, 151, 157, 160
"Tenor, The" (Andreev), 46, 163
Terioki, 106
Teternikov, F. K., see Sologub, Fëdor Kuz'mich
That Which Has Not Been (Savinkov), 185
"Thought" (Andreev), 12, 34, 36, 38, 41-42, 46, 47, 159, 161, 162
"Three, The" (Andreev), 39, 161
Tikhonov, A. N., 108, 110, 181
Timkovskii, N. I., 25, 153
To the Stars (Andreev; theme: "The Astronomer"), 77, 79, 173, 174
Today (Trachtenberg), 55
Tolstaia, Sof'ia Andreevna, 159
Tolstoy, Leo, 26, 32, 39, 70, 116, 125, 127, 128, 132, 157, 171, 179, 182
Trachtenberg, Vladimir Osipovich (Tararakhtenberg), 55, 167
Trepov, Dmitrii Fëdorovich, 68, 70, 171
Tret'iakovskii Gallery (Moscow), 49, 164
Trubetskoi Bastion, Fortress of Peter and Paul (St. Petersburg), 171
Truth (periodical), 28, 52, 53, 77, 155, 166

"Tsar, The" (Andreev), 53, 57, 72, 76, 77, 78, 90, 166, 173, 180
Tseitlin (shareholder in *Shipovnik* publishing house), 113, 140, 182
Turgenev, Ivan S., 18
Twain, Mark, 87, 176

United States, 12, 84, 85-87, 175, 176

Vasil'ev, Nikolai, 39
Vasilii, Father, 77, 142, 144
Veligorskaia, Alexandra Mikhailovna (also called Deaconess Alexandra; Lady Shura), 23, 45, 81, 90, 92, 95-96, 119, 122, 152, 159, 163, 176
Veresaev, Vikentii Vikent'evich (pseud. of V. V. Smidovich; also called Vikent'ich), 59, 116, 168
Verlaine, Paul, 93
Viatka, 122, 128, 183
Vikent'ich, *see* Veresaev, Vikentii Vikent'evich
Vinaver, Maksim Moiseevich, 74, 75, 173
Vinnichenko, Vladimir Kirillovich, 138, 187
Volga Herald (newspaper), 27
Vol'nov, Ivan Egorovich (pseud. I. Vol'nyi), 137, 138, 139
Vol'nyi, I. (pseud. of Ivan Egorovich Vol'nov), 137, 186
Volynskii (pseud. of Akim L'vovich Flekser), 138, 187

Volzhina, Ekaterina Pavlovna, 79, 173-174

"Wall, The" (Andreev), 31, 38, 40, 156
White Nights (magazine), 94, 178
"Will of the People" group, 4n
World (newspaper), 63, 169
World of Art (magazine and society), 164

Yalta, 17, 30, 32, 44, 73, 156, 172
Yesterday, Today, and Tomorrow (Trachtenberg), 55, 167

Zaitsev, Boris Konstantinovich, 94, 177
Zamula, Rudolph, 12n
Zhakov, K. F., 139, 187
Zinochka, *see* Hippius, Zinaida Nikolaevna
Zola, Emil, 57
Znanie (publishing house), 6, 26, 42, 50, 56, 63, 94, 99, 100, 108, 109, 113, 129, 132, 154, 155, 158, 162, 168, 169, 174, 175, 179, 182, 185
Znanie Literary Volumes, 103-4, 180; No. 1, 50, 160, 165-66; No. 1 and No. 2, 56, 167; No. 3, 170; No. 4, 171; No. 18, 176
Zolotarev, Aleksei, 139, 187